SOA ON THE WINGS OF COURAGE

The Art of Self-Encouragement

SOARING ON THE WINGS OF COURAGE

The Art of Self-Encouragement

OLAYINKA JOSEPH

GOLDEN HEART BOOKS

This book is available at a special discount when ordered in bulk quantities.
For information, Contact Ola Joseph
P.O. Box 721791, Houston Texas 77272-1791.
Tel: (713) 283-5141 or 1-800-522-1970

Copyright © 2001 by Olayinka Joseph
All rights reserved.
No part of this book may be reproduced, stored in a retrieval system, or transmitted by any means, electronic, mechanical, photocopying, recording, or otherwise, without written permission from the author.

ISBN 0-75962-114-4

This book is printed on acid free paper.

P.O.Box 721791, Houston TX 77272-1791.
(713) 283-5141 or 1-800-522-1970
Printed in the United States of America.

1stBooks – rev. 04/12/01

Praise for "Soaring On The Wings Of Courage"

"Sometimes it is too easy to forget who we are created to be, and to forget that challenges in life are the stepping stones to greater heights. *Soaring On The Wings of Courage* has given a prescription of courage to overcome and rise above limitations. To remain as you are denies who you can be."

    Dr. Ignatus Okeze
    Pastor/Speaker
    Author of Hope For Your Marriage

"A collection of stories and essays that will warm your heart and encourage your spirit."

    Dianna Booher
    Author of Communicate with Confidence and The Worth of a Woman's Words

"These simple, but inspiring stories can be used to lift your own spirits or give you a message about resiliency that you can pass on to someone you are mentoring."

    Dr. Shirley R. Peddy
    Author of The Art of Mentoring.

"Ola Joseph has given us a gift - a renewed vision of courage. With unforgettable stories and exhilarating applications, this book is a honest-to-goodness inspiration!"

    Rosie Horner
    Author of The Olympian Woman and 59 Ways to Show Our Clients We Care

"Ola Joseph's stories of courage and hope hit right to the heart of how to successfully meet and overcome the personal barriers and limitations that all of us encounter. An absolutely outstanding book!"

    Wayne G. Springer
    President, Atiwa Computing Inc.

"A must-read book that exhibits the difference between success and failure. Your life will never be the same again after reading this book."
   Dr. Abla Adadevoh
   Houston Community College

"Great inspiration and motivation to move anyone who reads it! Ola has a way of taking the negative circumstances in life and showing people how to turn them into positive outcomes. His words of wisdom are true and real"
   Christine Gautreau
   The Terrace

"*Soaring On The Wings of Courage* shows us that finding triumph in life takes the courage to face life's daily struggles head on. We would all do good to remember this message."
   Manny Garza
   Encouragement Research and Resources

"*Soaring On The Wings Of Courage* is a collection of brilliantly written and well organized inspirational stories. These stories highlight the God-given gifts inside each of us."
   Tola Oresusi
   Tola & Associates

"The stories shared in Ola Joseph's latest book, "*Soaring On The Wings of Courage*," are shining examples and wake-up-calls for each of us to search for the gold in all of life's lessons. This warm, easy-to-read book is packed full of inspiring, antidotal thoughts, ideas and ideals of hope and encouragement."
   Dan Maddux
   Executive Director/CEO
   American Payroll Association

"This is a book that gives the reader determination to triumph against all odds."
   Georgie Holbrook
   Author of Joy-Full Holistic Remedies

"Artful, informative, and delightful…Ola Joseph has gifted us with moving stories of comfort and promise that guide in cultivating our dreams and experiencing our possibilities."
Richard A. Griffin, Ph.D.

"As an advocate of inspiration and encouragement, I highly recommend you read and add to your collection of "good" books a copy of Ola Joseph's *Soaring On The Wings Of Courage*," for the title says it all."
Jerry A. Pruitt
Toastmasters International D.56 PRO

"Inspiring and enlightening, *Soaring on the Wings of Courage* is filled with charming stories that just might give its readers a new outlook on life."
Chaz Kyser
Editor of LaVida News

"The moral in the stories is strong enough to preach courage, determination, and purpose for life. I fully endorse your effort and enjoy the stories in Soaring on the Wings of Courage. Go ahead and write more books. They will lift up lives!"
Ade Osunneye
Retired Principal of Lagos City College, (Ola's alma mater)

Contents

Praise for "Soaring On The Wings Of Courage" i
Acknowledgements vii
Appreciation ix
Dedication xi
Introduction xiii

1. AN UNLIKELY MENTOR 1
2. I WON! 7
3. COME TO THE EDGE 12
4. A GOAL IS A DREAM WITH A TIMELINE 16
5. QUITING? NOT AN OPTION 21
6. HE WHO LAUGHS LAST 25
7. JUST CAN'T TAKE NO FOR AN ANSWER 30
8. THE POWER OF PURPOSE 42
9. STORING IMAGES FOR A LIFETIME 47
10. PATIENCE IS A VIRTUE 51
11. IF YOU THINK YOU CAN, YOU WILL 54
12. SHAKE IT OFF AND STEP UP 56
13. WHOSE HOUSE AM I BUILDING? 58
14. DON'T LEAVE HOME WITHOUT IT 60
15. THE HAPPIEST AND SADDEST DAY 62
16. TEACH A CHILD THE WAY HE SHOULD GO 64
17. ASK NOT WHAT GOD CAN DO FOR YOU 69
18. SUCCESS IS A JOURNEY 73

19. THE SPRINGBOARD OF LIFE	76
20. MOTHER IS SUPREME	79
21. PLAYING TO WIN OR PLAYING NOT TO LOSE?	82
22. HE THAT IS IN US	85
Other Contributors	95
OTHER TITLES BY OLAYINKA JOSEPH	97
ORDER FORM	99
ABOUT THE AUTHOR	101

Acknowledgements

Some very good friends looked at my first book and said, "You must write a sequel to that." Some even volunteered to share their stories in this new book.

I thank those who took my manuscripts and trudged their way through with suggestions and insights. I'll be forever indebted to you.

Appreciation

My warmest thanks go to all those who took time off their busy schedules to contribute stories to my book. Thanks for sharing your wonderful and heartfelt stories.

Many thanks to Dick Cummings for taking time to read through my manuscript and making useful suggestions for improvement.

Thanks to all those who read my manuscript and offered comments for endorsement.

My thanks also go to Chaz Kyser for editing the final draft and for her promotional reviews.

Dedication

This book is dedicated to every member of my immediate and extended family, and everyone that contributed the wonderful stories in the book.

Introduction

Life gives everybody lemons. Some squeeze them and bring out lemonade. That is courage!

In my first book, titled *"Voices of Courage-Everyone Has a Story"* you saw true life stories of everyday people who, through courage and faith in God, surpassed themselves and the expectations of others.

However, there is something about the people in "Soaring on the Wings of Courage" that appeals to my sense of purpose. They believe in possibilities, and they have an attitude of fortitude.

To appreciate the content of this new book, let me take you back to your kitchen.

Remember the last time you put your kettle on the stove and filled it up to the brim? What did the kettle do when the water began to boil? It started to sing. That is one of the characteristics of a kettle. It has a sweet attitude. When it is neck deep in hot water it sings and whistles.

The same goes for successful people. They have characteristics that give them a positive attitude towards life. They see an opportunity in every problem. When life gives them a lemon, they find a way to squeeze lemonade out of it.

These characteristics include faith, endurance, hope, perseverance, commitment, focus, purpose, dedication, a positive attitude, action, dependability, reliability, and other positive attributes.

The stories in this book will inspire you to get off your seat and take charge of your life using the God-given power that you already possess.

In God's great economy, nothing goes to waste. No matter what you want to do, if you have any of the characteristics highlighted in this book, you can make anything happen. If you don't already have all of them, you can develop them. As Maya Angelou rightly puts it, "Life loves to be taken by the lapel and told: I am with you, kid. Let's go."

Creating Our Unique Role As God's Emissaries

Through

C - Character

O - Opportunity

U - Understanding

R - Relationship

A - Action

G - Godliness

E - Enthusiasm

1

AN UNLIKELY MENTOR

"I've never met a person, I don't care what his condition, in whom I could not see possibilities…the capacity for reformation and change lies within."
- Preston Bradley

* * * * *

He was short and heavy-set, with a salt and pepper beard and twinkling blue eyes. Despite his extraordinary wealth and success, he insisted he wasn't a big shot…just a little shot that kept on shooting. Though our paths never crossed directly, his words and teachings have had a profound influence on how I approach my business. Our views on politics and religion held no common ground, and we parted ways in business years ago, but my respect and affection for him is boundless. His name is Dexter Yager.

The year was 1994 and I was not content with my life. After years in dead-end jobs as an administrative assistant, with excellent reviews but no college degree, I was tired. I wanted change, but I wasn't sure what that meant. If I went back to school, what would I study? The age-old question, "What do you want to be when you grow up?" was demanding an answer.

One night I awoke from a sound sleep to see the full moon filling my room with light. I watched it for a long time, and my lifelong dream of being a writer began to bubble up from some deep, forgotten place inside of me. I longed for the freedom to stay up at night to watch the moon, knowing that in the depth and stillness of the night I could hear the muse that my busy, stressful life had silenced.

I didn't know it at the time, but I was praying one of the most heartfelt prayers of my life. A few weeks later my husband and I were introduced to a business concept. Intrigued by what I heard, I wondered if this would be the path that would set me free from my job so I could live a writer's life.

We were given basic instructions on building our business: read 15 minutes a day from an inspirational book, listen to audiotapes, and attend seminars. My husband and I did this dutifully, and we began to learn from a master teacher.

Dexter talked about having a dream, and I knew I had mine. That was the easy part. What I had not learned was how to take that dream and turn it into reality. Dexter said that if we had our dream in our hearts, we could overcome any fears that stood in our way. Still, I struggled with my fears, finding it painful to approach people. We worked hard, but I was no closer to leaving my job and I grew ever more frustrated. Would I ever break through my self-imposed prison?

We kept reading, listening to tapes, and going to seminars. I felt smarter and better informed about business in general, but couldn't translate what I was learning into financial success. I often had trouble hearing what Dexter had to say, because his political and religious beliefs were so at odds with mine that I was often left fuming after one of his talks! Eventually, we had to admit that we had failed, and that it was time to move on.

Once Dexter gets in your head, though, there's no turning back. His teachings continued to work on us, and I remembered everything: dream big, find ways to hold the vision every day, find a reason to do what you're doing, and you will have the fuel to help you move beyond fear. I knew these principles would work if I persisted, no matter what business vehicle we used. Somehow, I would learn to use them successfully.

In the meantime, we were undergoing a series of crises that would test all of our beliefs. In the beginning of 1996 I became ill with a debilitating illness, followed closely by job losses for both my husband and me, and two unsuccessful pregnancies. I was reeling with grief and uncertainty. Each time I came up for air, I felt pushed into the deep waters again and I was fighting not to drown.

I remembered how Dexter had fought back from a stroke that had paralyzed one side of his body. He faced this challenge without self-pity. He used the adversity to propel him forward, to become better. Could I do the same thing?

I thought of Dexter as I struggled with the neurological symptoms that limited me, knowing that I would find a way to heal. Images of his determination kept me going, and I began to fight my way back. I found ways to work with my body and mind, and I was seeing results. I was physically weak, but my fighting spirit was beginning to emerge. My husband and I found lifelines to help us cope with losing our babies, including a local support group and books for bereaved parents. I felt myself growing internally in strength and character, knowing that there was no longer anything to fear, because I had survived the worst.

One day my mother and I were talking on the phone. She had been to a bookstore looking for a book for bereaved grandparents, and couldn't find one. "Would you help me?" she asked.

"Sure," I said. "No problem."

I was shocked to find, however, that no such book existed. There were only booklets and one book that was no longer in print. I was incensed! How could there be so many resources available for parents, and so few for the grandparents, who had to deal with the dual grief of losing a grandchild and watching their own bereaved children suffering, unable to help?

"There's nothing available," I told her. Then I added the words that changed my life, "I guess I'll do it."

I went to work fueled by pain and a sense of mission. I, who had talked about writing a book my whole life but had never put pen to paper to do so, wrote a draft in just a few months. My shyness didn't matter as I sought grandparents who were willing to be interviewed for the book.

I pushed my fear aside as I wrote to publisher after publisher, proposing my idea. Their rejections rolled off me like a cool spring rain. None of it mattered, the book would be published. Dexter had said that we must know why we are doing something to keep going in spite of obstacles. I finally had my "why," and so I knew that the "how" was not far behind.

Filled with the strength that comes from understanding one's purpose, I finally understood Dexter's words. This book had gotten into my heart, and there was no turning back. No amount of fear or rejection would stop me. I was learning to grow beyond dreaming, and to "put feet to my prayers," as he often said.

Deciding that seeking a publisher was a waste of time, I learned how to self-publish. In October of 1999, I held my book, *"When a Grandchild Dies: What to Do, What to Say, How to Cope,"* in my hands for the first time. It was a moment that felt much like giving birth, except that this time my "child" was very much alive. For the first time in my life I felt successful.

I knew that my life would be forever altered by this experience, and it has been. *"When a Grandchild Dies"* has been accepted into the catalogs of major bereavement organizations such as The Compassionate Friends, Centering Corporation, and A Place to Remember.

I introduced the book at the national conference of the Association of Death Education and Counseling, where I met many wonderful professionals who received it enthusiastically. I'm beginning to accept speaking engagements, and I'm working on several other books, both fiction and nonfiction. I've also edited another book, *Joy-Full Holistic Remedies: How to Experience Your Natural Ability to Heal* by Georgie Holbrook, which is receiving international acclaim and excellent reviews. My writing life is full and satisfying, and I work hard at improving my skills. Sometimes I have trouble believing that I am a professional author!

Olayinka Joseph

All this has happened, in part, because of what one funny little bearded man taught me. As time passes, my differences of opinion with Dexter no longer matter, and what I remember most are the gems of knowledge he so willingly gave me.

And sometimes at night, when the full moon fills my room with light, I remember the prayer of long ago, and I marvel at all that has come to pass. Dexter, wherever you are, thanks.

- Nadine Galinsky

2

I WON!

"Never tell a young person that something can not be done. God may have been waiting for centuries for somebody ignorant enough of the impossible to do that thing."
― Dr. J. A. Holmes

* * * * *

Have you ever experienced something that completely changed your thought process or perhaps even your entire set of values? If you have, I am confident that you would agree with me that it could be a humbling experience.

Despite this, I am equally confident that you may have some difficulty grasping the fact that a single episode in one's life can have such a dramatic impact. From personal experience I can assure you that it can and does happen.

In my case, until some time ago I was truly satisfied with what I had accomplished. I was not rich and famous but I had set some high goals and attained most of them.

For example, there was my navy career. I had enlisted in the navy in August of 1950. After recruit training and a stay at the enlisted submarine school in New London, I was assigned to a submarine for duty.

This exhilarating and somewhat unusual experience convinced me that I should pursue a navy career. The question then became one of deciding how I could maximize this decision. Being an enlisted man was a good start, but it was akin to being in a dog team – only the lead dog gets a change of scenery.

I wanted that change of scenery so I successfully applied for a fleet appointment to the Naval Academy. Four years later, I graduated and was commissioned an ensign.

After graduation I decided that a career as a naval aviator was the career path of choice. Once again, I was successful in being assigned to flight training.

Eighteen months later I received the coveted wings of gold and launched off into a successful career as a naval aviator. This allowed me to do some things that others equally or possibly even better qualified would never do. The reason for this was that they would not have the opportunity.

For instance, I logged more than 1,600 carrier landings. Well, actually, that is 1,599 landings and one flight deck crash. Since I crashed on the centerline and walked away from it, I counted this as a landing.

I had a deep feeling of satisfaction and pride at this point, yet I failed to realize that this feeling of euphoria had placed me in the same position as that of the man who jumped off the Empire State Building. As he passed the 72nd floor, he said "So far, so good!"

Then something happened. I heard a true story that changed everything. I am now going to relate this as if it had actually happened to me, and by doing so trust that this technique will help bring the saga to life for you.

The incident involved a track meet. Interestingly enough, it was not even a major event with world-class athletes. It was a simple local meet in San Diego.

I sat in Balboa Stadium, basking in the afternoon sun I was oblivious to what was soon to happen. The 100 yard dash event was announced, and my attention was directed to the head of the track where eight runners were struggling to get out of their warm up suits. I focused my attention on a young blonde girl who would be running in lane 6. Could this have been a premonition?

Finally, everyone was ready and the starter called the runners to the starting line. At the crack of the starter's pistol, the runners lurched forward.

It was immediately obvious that this was not going to be a Michael Johnson dash to a world record.

You see, the American Special Olympics Committee sponsored this meet. Each athlete was mentally or physically disabled to some degree or another.

As the runners approached the halfway point, four of them had dropped well back, but the young girl in lane 6 was still in contention. Then she too started to fade ever so slowly.

"How disappointing," I said to myself. I had been so confident that she would be in contention at the finish.

Then I saw a remarkable change take place. The girl's jaws tightened with determination. Her eyes blazed with a fierce competitive fire. She lengthened her stride, and inch by agonizing inch she clawed herself back into contention.

Then she pulled slightly ahead, and won the race.

After a round of hugs, the girl walked ever so slowly over to the stands and looked up to where her mother was sitting. With a shy smile and some hesitation, she simply said, " I won!"

Her mother brushed aside some tears, smiled, and said, "Yes my darling, you certainly did!"

As I watched this I was so moved that I had to go down to congratulate the mother. I said, "you must be very proud of your daughter."

The mother agreed - what mother wouldn't? She added, however, "...but you see, these tears of joy are not because Jeanette won the race. When Jeanette said, 'I won,' those were the first words that she had ever spoken!"

At that moment I knew that my entire life had changed. All of those accomplishments that had seemed to be so impressive had suddenly become nothing more than a mere footnote on the bottom of a page of mundane events.

Oh, I don't want to create the impression that I became discouraged – quite the contrary! I was now positively and enthusiastically motivated to do something that would help make this world a little better place to live.

In other words, I wanted to leave my footprints in the sands of time.

I am not sure at this point whether hearing that story has in fact enabled me to reach the new goals that I have set. I am not sure that I would have made any monumental change in the grand scheme of things if I were able to attain them all.

I do know one thing for sure. By striving in this manner, whenever anyone asks me how things are going, I can respond in the same manner, as did Jeanette -"**I WON!**"

- Dave Teachout

3

COME TO THE EDGE

"Come to the edge, he said...They said: We are afraid... Come to the edge, he said...They came...he pushed them...And they flew."
— *Guillaume Apollinaire*

* * * * *

Her name was Robin, and as a child she indeed seemed as frail as a young bird. And as she grew, life could have treated her better. Her teenage years found her alone with her divorced mother, whose job paid little and provided no medical insurance. In addition, there was no child support to help out.

Robin never finished high school. She went to work in a carwash to provide herself with clothes and transportation. In an all too familiar cycle, she ended up a divorced parent herself, with two kids to support and a dim future. This story could end here, however, it does not.

Robin had something a little extra going for her. One thing her mother accomplished with fierce determination was to instill in Robin an irrevocable belief that she could stand on her own and be and do anything she wanted, if she set her mind to it.

That is exactly what she did. Through family connections, she received a scholarship to a trade school. But there was one catch. To take advantage of it meant studying aircraft mechanics - a career that was hardly the dream of most young girls. However, it was a much-needed break and

Robin was not going to let it slip away. She was going to take advantage of it.

It was tough. Robin was the only female in her class. She took a lot of "stuff" from the guys. Would she be good enough to stack up and shoulder the load side by side with them? Many of them did not think so.

In October of 1990, she graduated, took her diploma, and went to work. She was the only female out in the hanger. Nevertheless, by now she was used to the barbs. She ignored them, toughened up a little more, and did her job.

With an employment offer that seemed ironclad, she packed up her kids and her few possessions and drove a U-Haul all the way from Colorado to Oregon. When she got there she found that the company was unable to honor its commitment to her.

The cruel hand of fate had struck once more. Again, she struck back. She called the local media and told her story on television. It was a story that played well, as she represented many others who had come from around the country with a promise of work at the same organization. Unlike her, many of them turned around and went home.

But, Robin had just spent all her money on an apartment for her and the children. There was nothing left to get her back home, and there was no job.

Within days of the broadcast, Robin's story touched an official from another airline based in the same city. He offered her a job interview and she got the job.

Battling single parenthood, homesickness, and the need to be "better than the guys" in a male-dominated field, Robin worked to establish herself. This meant long, grueling hours on the midnight shift, a scramble to find adequate babysitting through the night, and trying to sleep days with young children at home.

But it also meant something else. Robin had new self-esteem, and the freedom and confidence that come with realizing that you can go after your dreams and succeed.

Today, Robin helps keep the turbo props and jets of a major commuter airline flying and in good shape. She does everything from checking oil to replacing entire engines. In the early morning rush, she is often called upon to taxi an airplane from the hanger to the terminal. This requires handling a ten-million dollar aircraft across busy taxiways and a runway, all the while communicating with ground control. And because the airport is right next to a river, it often takes place in a blanket of fog! Robin's knowledge, experience, and careful attention to detail are a few of the reasons you can step on an airplane and know that you are on one of the safest forms of transportation in the world.

Robin is raising her children with the same philosophy that was passed on to her the only limitations on our destiny are the ones we place on ourselves. If each of her children follows what she has taught them and what they have seen by example, they will never lack the wisdom to stand up for themselves.

Soaring on the Wings of Courage:
The Art of Self Encouragement

Her daughter will never doubt her own ability to pursue any career she can dream of. Likewise, her son will know that a real man never walks away from his responsibilities once he has chosen to become a father.

The girl with no future has become a woman with unlimited potential. Robin is without a doubt an inspiration.

Is something holding you back? Are you a single parent, stuck in a job that is going nowhere? Are you alone, and afraid of the future? You can step above it all. I hope Robin's story helps inspire you to do just that.

Come to the edge. You can fly!

- *Carol Taylor*

4

A GOAL IS A DREAM WITH A TIMELINE

"Make the most of today. Translate your good intentions into actual deeds… Keep a definite goal of achievement constantly in view. Realize that work well and worthily done makes life truly worth living."
— *Grenville Kleiser*

* * * * *

When I was a young boy living in my small village back in Nigeria, I used to play football (soccer) matches with friends. We played in any open space we could find.

Most of the time the space would be just large enough to be a living room. At times it would be a space between two buildings, or even on the main street.

The most interesting thing about this is that as young as we were, somehow we knew the importance of setting goals. During these so-called matches, we used to look for poles, stones, or bricks. Sometimes all we could do was to draw two parallel lines to indicate where the goal posts should have been or were supposed to be.

In fact, I recall several occasions when we had members of one team take off their shirts and place them in piles on the ground to mark where the goals were supposed to be.

Without goals we would not have known what to shoot for, or at worst, we would not have been able to keep score.

I have seen basketball players play from one end of the court to the other in recent times. Sometimes I wonder what it would look like if there were no baskets to shoot for. No doubt the whole game would be boring and confusing.

The importance of goal setting cannot be overemphasized. In order for anyone to measure his progress, to know whether he is moving in the right direction, he must set goals. For an individual to live an outstanding life, he needs to set goals.

The Importance of Setting Goals

When I wrote my first book, *"Voices of Courage-Everyone Has a Story,"* I set a goal to have the book published and released by the spring of 2000.

I completed the book, but no publisher was ready to take it. Those who were willing to publish it had a period of 18 to 24 months turnaround. That was not acceptable to me, so I decided to go out on a limb and publish my book myself. My book came out in the spring of 2000 as planned.

In setting a goal, I have discovered that the most important question I need to ask is "How can a man hit a target he can't see?" In the example given above about soccer matches, you might ask how we could have known when the ball went into the net without having goal posts.

It is now clear that goals provide you with a distinct picture, a sense of control and assurance that you are actually moving in the right direction. When you choose your goals and follow them religiously, you have a clear-cut picture of your destination and you have a way to measure your progress.

This is definitely common with successful people. They set goals and follow them religiously. If there are problems, they make slight adjustments and continue with their tasks.

Characteristics of Goal Setting

What do you want to achieve? The first thing you have to do is decide what you really want to achieve. It has been said that, "if you don't know where you are going, any road will take you there."

By deciding what you set out to achieve, you have a destination. Then you can start to work on how to get there. A journey of ten thousand miles starts with the first step, and knowing where you want to go helps to determine which direction you will turn.

Oliver Wendell Holmes once said *"the greatest thing in this world is not so much where we are, but in what direction we are moving."* You are either moving towards your goal or away from it.

The mathematicians would say that the shortest distance between two points is a straight line. Having a goal and moving towards that goal provides an opportunity to move in a straight line, which makes the journey shorter, more visible, and less painful.

Time Factor: When you set a goal, you must attach a specific period of time in which you expect to accomplish the set goal. If there is no time limit attached to your goal, it is simply not a goal. Anyone can write something on a piece of paper as a goal and take forever to accomplish it.

As the quotation at the beginning of this chapter states, *"a goal is a dream with a timeline."* When a time limit is attached, there is a sense of purpose.

Your goal must be measurable: A goal must be measurable in one form another. It could be measured in terms of how much money is to be made during a certain period, or a number of pounds to lose in weight.

Whatever your goals are, there must be a way to measure your progress towards them.

Write it down: Writing a goal down lends credence to the fact that the goal-setter is serious about what he/she wants to achieve. How can you remember your goals without having them written down on paper or entered as data in an electronic device that will remind you at regular intervals?

If you believe in the Bible, you are probably familiar with Isaiah 8:1 *"Moreover the Lord said unto me, 'take thee a great roll, and write in it with man's pen concerning Maher-shalal-hash-baz.'"*

Another passage that enjoins us to write things down is Proverbs 3:3 *"…bind them about thy neck; write them upon the table of thine heart."*

Without writing down what you want to accomplish, the goal only exists as a figment of your imagination, and there is every likelihood that you will forget. When it is written down; however, it becomes something tangible, something that can be seen, felt, and touched. It keeps it in sight all the time.

It must be achievable: Setting a goal so high that it is not within reach can be as useless as not having a goal at all. It will be foolhardy for me to set a goal to save $10,000 in six months if my income is only $15,000 a year. To make a goal achievable, it must be realistic or else it will lead to frustration and disappointment.

Long and Short-Range Goals: Just as there are short-range goals, there are long-range goals. One of the best ways of looking at this aspect is to set small short-range goals that you can achieve. Set a goal that you can see, and when you have achieved it set another one, maybe a little higher than the first one.

Goal setting is an essential ingredient in reaching for greater heights. To soar to greater and higher heights, you have to set goals higher than the previous ones. That way, there is always something to aspire to and something to reach for.

Remember, goal setting is one of the basic ingredients of a successful career. Those who fail to plan, plan to fail. If you set no goals, you have no plans; if you have no plans, you plan to work for someone who has one.

If I had not set goals as to when I wanted my book published and released, I probably would still be waiting for a publishing house today.

Goal setting is one of the characteristics of highly successful people, and anyone who aspires to succeed must know what he/she wants and set achievable, realistic goals with a time line.

- Ola Joseph

5

QUITING? NOT AN OPTION

"Be like a postage stamp. Stick to something until you get there."

- Josh Billings.

* * * * *

Ever since I was twelve years old, I knew I wanted to become a clinical psychologist. I did not know what that meant entirely, but I knew I would help people. This desire was reinforced by my ninth grade English teacher, who commented on a creative writing assignment that I had great insight into the human psyche. That was all I needed to hear.

When many high school students were still exploring career possibilities, I knew what I wanted to be. When other high school students were living for the moment, I had a plan of action: 1) I would attend a four-year institution; 2) I would go on to graduate school and; 3) I would become a clinical psychologist.

It was impressed upon me early that clinical psychology programs were highly competitive, and that I would need to do well in my classes and distinguish myself as a serious student. With this in mind, I became determined to make the best possible grades. Many of my academic goals were accomplished, including studying at Oxford University, becoming a member of Phi Beta Kappa, and graduating with university and departmental honors. I accomplished the first step toward becoming a clinical psychologist without a hitch. However, the second step proved to be more elusive.

I was not accepted into a clinical psychology doctoral program immediately after college. Well-meaning graduate admissions departments encouraged me to apply to doctoral programs in counseling and educational psychology, but that was not part of my plan. Instead, I entered a masters program, and two years later I reapplied to doctoral programs in clinical psychology. This time I was met with success, and was on my way to completing the third step of my goal, or so I thought.

Doctoral study proved to be more challenging than I anticipated. Even though I had a long history of academic success, I was not prepared to tackle graduate statistics. The plan that I had made many years ago hinged on passing this class. In graduate school, grades below "B" are unacceptable, so when it became clear that I would make a "C" in the course, I withdrew. The department did not look upon this favorably, and it was made clear to me that I had to pass this course. Dropping the course, a second time was not an option. The fear of failure overwhelmed me to the point that I considered taking a year-long sabbatical from the program to prepare for the statistics course.

While visiting my parents during the summer break, I told them about this new wrinkle in my plan. My mother stared at me sympathetically, but my father's immediate response was, "Where do you plan to live during your sabbatical?"

I responded, "You mean I can't stay here?"

At this point, Daddy reminded me that my "home" was a thousand miles away and then he said something that has been etched in my memory ever since. "If you start running from problems now, you'll be running for the rest of your life," he advised.

I was disappointed about the prospect of facing possible failure, but I readied myself to go back. As I finished packing, I could hear the pecking of typewriter keys, but I did not pay it much attention. Unknown to me, Daddy had taken the time to type a poem from the church bulletin. He handed it to me just as I was leaving. It read as follows:

Storms Bring Out the Eagles, but the Little Birds Take Cover

When the storms of life gather darkly ahead,
I think of the wonderful words I once read
And I say to myself as threatening clouds hover
Don't fold up your wings and run for cover
But, like the eagle, spread wide your wings and soar far above the troubles life brings
For the eagle knows that the higher he flies,
The more tranquil and brighter become the skies ...
And there is nothing in life God ever asks us to bear
That we can't soar above on the Wings of Prayer
And in looking back over the storm you passed through
You'll find you gained strength and new courage too,
For facing life's storms with an eagle's wings
You can fly far above earth's small, petty things.

- Helen Steiner Rice

The date written on the sheet of paper containing the poem is August 14, 1983. As I look at the framed poem that sits on my office desk, I realize that a lot has happened since then. Not only did I complete step three of my action plan but I became an associate professor at a Christian university. I find it ironic that one of the courses I have taught at this and two other institutions is statistics.

Several fitting clichés could serve as the moral for my story. One is "plan your work and work your plan" and the other is "failure is endeavor, and endeavor persisted in is never a failure." However, I think Winston Churchill said it best, "Never give up!"

- Renata L. Nero, Ph.D.

6

HE WHO LAUGHS LAST

"He that stays focused never stub his toes."

- Ola Joseph

* * * * *

In the ancient time in most countries of Africa, it was the responsibility of the parents to find fitting partners for their grown sons and daughters.

Several years ago there was a king who ruled over a small kingdom. The king had a beautiful daughter named Nike, who was of marriageable age.

This king sent out word that his daughter was of age and ready to marry, and that all eligible young men in the kingdom should come to the palace for a marriage contest. Whoever prevailed would have the girl for a wife.

On the appointed day, all the eligible young men in the kingdom went to the palace. The contest included wrestling, boxing, catching the biggest fish, and hunting.

At the end of the day, only two young men remained in the contest, as all the others had dropped out.

There was one more thing for the two men to do before one of them could become the king's son-in-law.

There were special regalia to be worn by the bridegroom on the wedding day. The regalia were called "ewu-etu." This is similar to the tuxedo that bridegrooms wear in the western world.

In order to get this regalia, the two young men had to travel about sixty miles to another village where the man in custody of the regalia lived. These two young men were prohibited from using any means of transportation.

In other words, they had to run or walk. But it did not matter how long it took them. The person who returned to the village with the regalia was going to get the king's daughter for a wife.

The two young men ran side by side for several miles, putting aside the fact that they were competing against each other. They drew strength by keeping each other company.

However, as they came within ten miles of their destination, the one that was stronger, faster, and swifter took off in a sprint, leaving the other to eat the dust.

He ran so fast that he got to the chief's house several hours ahead of the other man. He was very happy that he was in good physical condition. He was sure that he was going to get the king's daughter for a wife.

He arrived to find the chief hosting a big party. There was a lot to eat and drink, and many people were dancing.

Tired as this young man was, his happiness was evident, and he decided to join in the merriment to celebrate his achievement of getting to the chief's house first.

He joined the party, ate good food and he drank and danced.

Meanwhile, the other young man was struggling to remain on his feet as he became tired, weary, thirsty, and hungry. He stumbled and fell several times.

At one point he decided to rest for a while, but he became unhappy because he was sure his opponent had won the contest by beating him in the race to get the regalia. But he continued, hoping that at least he would put up an appearance.

As he came within a mile of the chief's house, he heard a loud cheer and the sound of drums and clapping. His heart sank because he thought that it was useless for him to continue, since the cheer could have only meant that his opponent had received the regalia. On second thought, he decided to go see what it looked like in the chief's house.

When he eventually crashed in through the door, barely able to keep his eyes open, he felt drained and drenched in his sweat. His wobbled knees were too weak to support his weight.

The chief came to welcome him. He offered him food and drink, but the young man refused because he was unhappy that he could not get the king's daughter for a wife. He just simply shook his head, as he was too weak even to speak.

Eventually he was rested enough, and when he could speak he thanked the chief and expressed disappointment at himself for not being able to get there first to claim the regalia meant for the wedding of the king's daughter.

The chief told him that he was the first, but the man couldn't understand. He said, "but my opponent has been here, what do you mean I'm the first?"

The chief then asked him to wait while he went into his room to bring the "ewu-etu."

At this time, the first man became aware that the second man had arrived, and noticed that the chief was holding the regalia and about to give it to him. The second man was still dazed and astonished at the possibility of him getting the regalia even though he came second. He needed an explanation.

The first man voiced his objection and protested, claiming that he got to the chief's house first.

The chief told him to be quiet, and explained to him that he did not say why he was there, but instead just joined the party. He ate, drank, and danced, and since he considered the party more important than what he came for originally, he might as well enjoy it to the fullest.

In short, the regalia were handed to the second man, who eventually got the king's daughter for a wife.

The moral of this story is that the crown does not always go to the strongest, or the fastest or the swiftest. The crown goes to the man who remains focused on his purpose and does not give up even when it looks like all is lost. It is not over until it is all over.

Focus is the hallmark of all successful people. Once they decide on what they want and know how to get it, they never allow themselves to be derailed. Even if they are side-tracked, they remain focused until they achieve the purpose for which they set out to accomplish.

- Ola Joseph

7

JUST CAN'T TAKE NO FOR AN ANSWER

"Failure is only postponed success as long as courage 'coaches' ambition. The habit of persistence is the habit of victory."
- Herbert Kaufman

* * * * *

Some people take no for an answer and thereby miss the opportunity to reach their goal or achieve their purpose.

It is true that God provides food for the bird, but He will not put the food in its nest. The bird will have to go out and search for the food and bring it into its nest.

Persistence is the ability to keep trying no matter how much difficulty you are facing or who is rejecting you. A man who is persistent never takes no for an answer. To a persistent man, "no" means "not today, maybe tomorrow."

I joined Texaco Nigeria Limited in the mid 1980s and worked with Texaco until June 1990.

One morning in April of 1990, I came to the office at about 6:30 a.m., as usual. Five minutes later, I received a call from the security desk that I had a visitor.

I was surprised for two reasons. One, it was early in the morning and I had not given anyone an appointment. The office would not open until 8:00 a.m.

Second, I wondered how the person knew that I usually arrived that early. Or was it just a fluke?

Anyway, I went down to the security desk only to find my friend Mueyiwa waiting for me.

I had met Mueyiwa at the Nigerian National Petroleum Corporation in 1986 when we both went for a job interview. We had remained in contact ever since.

I was very curious, as her office was about five miles on the other side of the Lagos Downtown.

I asked what brought her to my office that early in the morning, since she had never visited my office before, although she knew where I worked.

She told me that she was no longer working at her former job at First City Merchant Bank, but knew there was an opening that I might be interested in and had come to inform me so I could file an application. She even gave me the name of the contact person.

I was happy that my persistence at staying in touch with Mueyiwa was yielding good results.

Over the years I had remained in contact by phone and occasional visits to her office, although she had never returned any of my calls or paid me a visit.

Anyway, that was the beginning of what became a life and death matter for me. In the next three months that followed, my persistence was put to test. My life was threatened, my potential was called into question, and my patience was vigorously tested.

That day I called the contact person, who asked me to bring my resume and other papers the following day.

When I got there the following day, he was impressed with my qualifications and experience. He said that he was going to set up a test for me. He felt that I was well qualified for the position, and that even if I couldn't get in at that point, it would be possible to get a chance at another time. This was good news for me.

The following week I took the test and passed. The woman who conducted the test, Mrs. Bisola Adekusibe, was highly impressed with my performance and said so when I called to check my results a few days later. She told me I had done very well and that I would hear from the administrative department very soon.

However, before I heard from the administrative department, I had been diagnosed with an inflamed appendix.

The day I was to go in for my surgery was the day I received a letter from the bank asking me to appear for an interview the following day. I had to make a critical decision between going in for surgery that night or waiting until the following day after the interview.

You guessed it. I did not show up for the surgery. I decided to postpone it.

If you're a man and you have received a blow below the belt before, then you can identify with the pain I was experiencing as I sat through the interview. I had to use my right hand to support the lower right side of my stomach. It felt like it would burst open at any minute.

I managed to endure the pain while I went through the interview. In retrospect, I am not sure whether the excruciating pain I was experiencing showed on my face or not. If it did, the three people who conducted the round table interview did not seem to notice, or just didn't care about my body language.

That afternoon I went back to my office at Texaco, cleared my desk, then went home to prepare for my surgery. It was now more than twenty hours delayed. During this time, I was experiencing terrible pain. Nevertheless, it was worth it to me. What I didn't realize was that I was toying with my life.

I went in for surgery and two days later while still recuperating from surgery, which was a life and death matter, (*a subject of another story*), I received yet another letter from the bank inviting me to come for an interview to discuss pay and other details. So I thought.

* * *

A little digression here.

I called the surgery a life and death matter because of what happened in the operating room. During the surgery, my body had reacted badly to the anesthesia. Here is what happened, according to my doctors and nurses.

I woke up in the middle of the operation and engaged the medical crew in a battle. Even though I was still drugged out, I was fighting with everyone and everything, I broke the restraining belts and more than eight additional people were called in to pin me down while the doctors performed the surgery. I couldn't remember anything, but the bruises on my hands, legs, and other parts of my body told the story for several weeks after the surgery.

That experience has led me to be apprehensive of any form of anesthesia or surgery.

Seven years later when I was a sailor in the United States Navy, my doctors suggested the possibility of correcting the bulging disk in my neck and my right Ulnar nerve through surgery. Naturally, I was very reluctant and it was with great trepidation that I agreed to have my arm operated upon. But even though the surgery went smoothly, it corrected nothing. It only succeeded in leaving a scar for me to remember yet another horrifying and tense moment of my life.

Don't forget why I'm telling you this story. I am talking about persistence and how much risk some of us are willing to take to get what we want.

Now back to the original story.

* * *

From my sickbed, I sent a note to the bank that I had gone into surgery shortly after leaving the interview that previous Thursday. I got a message back that I should come when I got out of the hospital.

Against my doctor's advice, I left the hospital a day before the 1990 World Cup in Italy. There were two reasons for my insisting on going home.

The first was that I wanted to watch the World Cup opening ceremony and record it on my color television. The set in my hospital room was a black and white set. In addition, I wanted to go home so I could go to the bank to negotiate my salary and other benefits.

I left the hospital on Thursday afternoon. The World Cup started on Friday, and the following Monday I went to the bank to negotiate my salary, though still weak from the surgery and the effects of the pain-relieving drugs.

One would think that when a salary has been negotiated and agreed upon, that one can have reasonable assurance of getting the position. Why would an employer negotiate a salary and agree upon a figure with the potential employee if he does not intend to give him a position?

Now this is where my level of persistence was greatly put to test. The utmost test!

A week after the salary negotiation, I went to the bank to follow up. To my surprise, no one knew what was happening. Suddenly the contact person was not prepared to talk to me any more. The people who had conducted the interview and negotiated the salary with me developed cold feet. The receptionist made a series of excuses. I went away when I couldn't wait any longer.

The following week, I called to check on what was happening. I was met with the same brick wall. No one in the administrative department seemed to know anything. This seemed strange to me.

Putting on my persistence cap, I decided to call on Mrs. Bisola Adekusibe, who conducted my test in the first place. She told me what I already knew. I had done well on the test and the administrative department would contact me later. That was good news for a change. I did not inform her about the experience I had had with the administrative department.

Two weeks later I was back at Mrs. Adekusibe's office. My reason or excuse? I was just in the area and decided to stop by to say hello. But my hidden objective was to remind her that I was still waiting in the wings and that I wasn't going to be put off easily. This time a surprise was waiting for me.

As soon as I was announced, she came out, and before I could speak, she said, "wait for me." She turned and went back to her office and came back with a typed sheet of paper. On the paper was a list of names including mine with a green check mark. She said, "What is this?" pointing at my name.

"That's my name," I said.

"What is this?" she asked, pointing at the green check mark.

"A check mark," I said feeling like a little child.

"That's the chairman's pen," she said "and it means that the chairman has recommended you for employment," she continued. "The last step before you are brought on board is for you to see the chairman. You will be contacted when the chairman is ready to see you. So don't get worked up. Go back to your office and continue with your present work until you are called. Your employment here is already guaranteed, it is just a matter of time," she said with the authority of someone who knew exactly what she was doing.

She added as an afterthought, "If by this time in two weeks you've not heard from us, come back and see me." With that, she disappeared into her cozy, well-furnished office.

I was floating in the air, so glad that I forgot to eat lunch that afternoon.

Perhaps you are wondering why I was so persistent.

By this time I was tired of working at Texaco. I needed something more challenging and more rewarding.

You see, when you are tired of something, you will do whatever it takes to move forward. It is crazy to complain about your situation without doing anything to change it. You cannot continue to do things the same way and expect a different result.

Moreover, the salary negotiation revealed that I was going to get about four times my salary at Texaco. If that was not enough to be excited about, I do not know what could be.

Two days after my last visit to Mrs. Adekusibe's office, I returned from work and found a letter in my letterbox. Usually, letters from the bank were hand delivered by dispatch riders, but this one had been mailed. That was unusual and it immediately aroused my curiosity.

I had been taught to look for things that were out of place, things that were unusual, or things that did not follow the normal pattern of behavior.

The opening paragraph of the letter said it all. It confirmed my fears. *"We regret to inform you..."*

To say I was enraged would be an understatement. Fortunately, my younger sister and my girlfriend were away at the time, so I had nobody to vent my anger, frustration, and disappointment on.

I looked at the signature and saw that the letter had come from the administration department. The administrative manager had signed it.

That night was the longest night of my life. I just couldn't understand the contradiction between what Mrs. Adekusibe had told me in confidence and the letter.

Should I confront the administrative manager? Did he disapprove of me? Was that why everyone from his department had tried to avoid talking to me, even though they had negotiated the salary package with me? What went wrong and where? If only I could find someone to tell me.

Only a few days ago, the personal assistant to the chairman had told me that I had been recommended for employment. Did she say that to keep me from coming to bother her? I could not answer any of these questions.

The following day was a Friday. I went to my office at Texaco and just moved around like a zombie. I felt deflated and angry all through the weekend. But I was determined to find out what was going on.

I headed straight for the bank during my lunch break on Monday. You guessed right, to Mrs. Adekusibe's office. By now everyone on her floor had seen so much of me that they knew who I was looking for as soon as I walked in. In fact, I overhead one of them saying, "Mrs. A's boyfriend is here."

As a matter of fact, on that day I did not fill out the usual visitor's form because the beautiful lady at the tenth floor reception desk had called Mrs. Adekusibe before I said a word. Whether she did it out of annoyance because of my incessant visits or because she was just doing her job, I don't know, but I was glad she did it. In retrospect, I am not sure how I would have sounded if I had had to speak. At that point, I was like a keg of gunpowder ready to explode.

When Mrs. Adekusibe came out, her eyebrows were up as if saying, "you again? What is it now?

You see, when you are persistent, people know right away that they can't shake you off. If you are persistent enough, you get what you want for sure.

I simply handed her the letter without a word and waited for her reaction. After reading through the letter, she smiled and shook her head. Then I spoke. "I'm not here to pin you down to what you told me in confidence, but I just wanted to see if you were aware of the letter."

Without a word, she went into her office, made a copy and gave me back the original (*which I still have today*) "If by this time next week you haven't heard from us come back," she said.

I thought that sounded familiar. However, I didn't say anything. I knew that I had a friend in her, and I didn't want her to feel that I didn't trust her.

Well, two days later, just after I returned from work, I heard a familiar sound - the sound of a motorbike. Minutes later my doorbell rang. I peered out to see who it was. It was a dispatch rider from First City Merchant

Bank and he had a letter for me. The content? You guessed right again. I was to report to the administrative manager's office at 10:00 a.m. the following day.

What's happening? How come a *"We regret to inform..."* suddenly changed to *"You are hereby requested to report...?"* Interestingly enough, the same man had signed both letters.

Someone said, "Be careful not to utter dirty words, because you may need to eat them later."

The good news is that on Monday, August 6, 1990, I walked into the bank as a fulltime employee. By December 31, 1990, the administrative manager who had been playing pranks with my career was gone.

* * *

You see, there is a story of how they catch monkeys in Brazil. They put a paw in a transparent bottle. The monkey can see the paw. When he puts his hand in the bottle and grabs the paw, he cannot bring out his hand. His hand would come out if he let go of the paw, but the monkey is too greedy and too hungry to let go. He struggles until the hunter or whoever set the trap comes along.

The unfortunate end of the administrative manager's career with the bank is not my purpose for narrating this story. The purpose for telling this story is to show that if you are persistent enough and willing to give it your all, you will get what you want. In my case, I was willing to give my life.

I gave it my all, I risked all, I remained undaunted by my unknown adversaries, and I got what I wanted. If anything had been held back at the time if I had failed to follow up and follow through, if I had not persisted and persevered I would not have had the opportunity to work at the bank. If I had not worked at the bank, I would not have been in the right place, and if I had not been in the right place, I would not have come to America. If I hadn't come to America, you would probably not be reading this story right now.

Take a lesson from my experience. What is it that you want right now that you don't have? Are you giving it all you have? If not, you need to ask yourself how badly do you want it? Are you willing to do what it takes to get it? Go for it.

Always remember that "no" means "not now, maybe tomorrow, maybe next month, or maybe next year." If you don't have what you need now, God is probably testing your level of persistence to see if you really want it that bad.

- Ola Joseph

8

THE POWER OF PURPOSE

"The purpose of life is to believe, to hope, and to strive."
                                                    - Indira Gandhi

* * * * *

There was a story told many years ago about an elementary school teacher. Her name was Mrs. Fillbrandt.

As Mrs. Fillbrandt stood in front of her fifth grade class on the very first day of school, she told the children a lie.

Like most teachers, she looked at her students and said that she loved them all equally. However, that was impossible, because there in the front row, slumped in his seat, was a little boy named Teddy Stoddard.

Mrs. Fillbrandt had watched Teddy the year before and noticed that he didn't play well with the other children, that his clothes were messy and that he constantly needed a bath. Moreover, Teddy could be unpleasant. She expected him to be the same in her class.

During the school year it got to the point where Mrs. Fillbrandt would actually take delight in marking his papers with a broad red pen, making bold X's and then putting a big "F" at the top of his papers.

At the school where Mrs. Fillbrandt taught, she was required to review each child's past records and she put Teddy's off until last. However, when she reviewed his file, she was in for a surprise.

Teddy's first grade teacher wrote, *"Teddy is a bright child with a ready laugh. He does his work neatly and has good manners...he is a joy to be around."*

His second grade teacher wrote, *"Teddy is an excellent student, well-liked by his classmates, but he is troubled because his mother has a terminal illness and life at home must be a struggle."*

His third grade teacher wrote, *"His mother's death has been hard on him. He tries to do his best, but his father doesn't show much interest, and his home life will soon affect him if some steps aren't taken."*

Teddy's fourth grade teacher wrote, *"Teddy is withdrawn and doesn't show much interest in school. He doesn't have many friends and sometimes sleeps in class."*

By now, Mrs. Fillbrandt realized the problem and was ashamed of herself. She felt even worse when her students brought her Christmas presents wrapped in beautiful ribbons and bright paper, all except Teddy.

His gift was clumsily wrapped in the heavy, brown paper that he got from a grocery bag. Mrs. Fillbrandt took pains to open it in the middle of the other presents. Some of the children started to laugh when she found a rhinestone bracelet with some of the stones missing and a bottle that was one quarter full of perfume. But she stifled the children's laughter when she exclaimed how pretty the bracelet was. She put on the bracelet and dabbed some of the perfume on her wrist.

Teddy Stoddard stayed after school that day just long enough to say, "Mrs. Fillbrandt, today you smelled just like my Mom used to." After the children left she cried for an hour.

On that very day, she quit teaching reading, writing, and arithmetic. Instead, she began to teach children. Mrs. Fillbrandt paid particular attention to Teddy.

As she worked with him, his mind seemed to come alive. The more she encouraged him, the faster he responded. By the end of the year Teddy had become one of the smartest children in the class, and despite her lie that she would love all the children the same, Teddy became one of her "pets."

A year later she found a note under her door from Teddy. He said that she was the best teacher he ever had in his whole life.

Six years went by before she got another note from Teddy. He wrote that he had finished high school third in his class, and she was still the best teacher he ever had in his whole life.

Four years after that she got another letter. He said that while things had been tough at times, he had stayed in school, had stuck with it, and would soon graduate from college with the highest honors. Teddy assured Mrs. Fillbrandt that she was still the best teacher he had ever had in his whole life.

Then four more years passed, and yet another letter came. This time Teddy explained that after he got his bachelor's degree, he decided to go a little further. Of course, the letter explained that Mrs. Fillbrandt was still the best teacher he had ever had. The letter was signed, Theodore F. Stoddard, M.D.

The story doesn't end there. There was yet another letter that spring. Teddy said he had met a girl and was going to be married. He explained that his father had died a couple of years ago, and he was wondering if Mrs. Fillbrandt might agree to sit in the place at the wedding that was usually reserved for the mother of the groom. Of course, Mrs. Fillbrandt did.

And guess what? She wore the bracelet he gave her, the one with several rhinestones missing. She also made sure she was wearing the perfume that Teddy remembered his mother wearing on their last Christmas together.

They hugged each other and Dr. Stoddard whispered in Mrs. Fillbrandt's ear, "Thank you, Mrs. Fillbrandt, for believing in me. Thank you so much for making me feel important and showing me that I could make a difference."

Mrs. Fillbrandt's eyes filled with tears. She said, "Teddy, you have it all wrong. You were the one who taught me that I could make a difference. I didn't know how to teach until I met you."

Never underestimate the Power of Purpose.

Having a purpose is much more important than having a plan. For one to be regarded as successful, he must have found his purpose in life and perform to the best of his ability.

Before there is a plan, there is a purpose. In other words, purpose precedes plan. You only start to plan after you have a purpose. Most successful people are purposeful people.

A man without a purpose is a wandering generalist. However, I strongly believe that there is no man living, even if he is on his deathbed, that has no purpose. Every man has a purpose for being alive. The only thing is to find it.

You see, before we were born, God had a purpose for us. Each of us has a purpose for being born into this world and each one of us is unique. The Bible says "...I am fearfully wonderfully made...(Psalm 139:14)

One interesting thing about purpose is that no one can help another carry out his purpose in life. You are the only one that is equipped to carry out your purpose. You have been created to serve a particular, unique purpose. For you to be successful, you must, like all successful people, find your purpose and go out to achieve it.

- Anonymous

9

STORING IMAGES FOR A LIFETIME

"I have not been able to find a single useful institution which has not been founded either by an intensely religious man or by the son (or daughter) [1] of a praying father or a praying mother."
- Roger W. Babson

* * * * *

"**J**udi, there is no gentle way to say this, but you are going blind."

I sat there suspended in space. The air rushed out of my lungs, and that one word played repeatedly in my head. ***BLIND! BLIND! BLIND!***

Fifteen years ago I went for a routine eye checkup. I knew I was failing the test when the doctor asked what line I could read on the eye chart. I looked around the room and said, "What eye chart?"

I just knew he was going to try to sell me new glasses. However, new glasses were not an option. Not any longer. I walked out of his office in a daze and went home and cried. I screamed. How could I possibly live as a blind person?

I cried. I cried until I was exhausted. I cried until I couldn't cry another tear. I knew I had two options. I could continue to feel sorry for myself and make everyone around me as miserable as I was, or I could accept what was happening, make the most of things until I was completely blind, and then find a good blind school to teach me how to live in a dark world.

I decided the second option was best. I started making a list of all the places I wanted to see. If I was going blind, I had better make the most of every moment.

We lived a short distance from Disneyland at the time and there was a fireworks display every night. Every night for a whole week, I went outside to watch.

Before I went blind, I wanted to see as much as I could of this beautiful country. My eyes were getting worse every day. In just a few short weeks I was totally blind in the dark. I couldn't leave my home at night without someone to guide me. I had to see as much as possible.

I started getting up at the crack of dawn to watch the sunrise. I studied flowers and trees. I studied pictures of friends and family, etching every line into my mind. I was storing up images to last a lifetime.

As I traveled with my husband he described the scenery we were passing. He compared it to other areas I had seen so I could picture it in my mind.

In the panhandle of Texas we passed cotton fields. Since I had never seen cotton growing, we stopped. I needed to get a closer look. I was on my knees looking at the pods. They had just started to open and the cotton was visible.

"What are you doing?" I saw a rifle pointed at me. I may not have been able to see very well, but I saw that gun. The barrel was at least two feet wide. The owner of the field was on the other end, and he was not happy. I quickly explained why I was kneeling in his field. I never took my eyes off that gun! He finally lowered the gun and took us on a tour.

He showed us how they pick and process the cotton, something I would never have seen had it not been for my eye problems.

By this time I had lost 95 percent of my sight in the light and 100 percent in the dark. So many things that I had taken for granted all my life were gone. No longer could I go for a walk by myself, go to the corner store for a quart of milk, watch TV or read a newspaper. I could no longer recognize my friends except by their voices.

I wanted to have more tests done on my eyes to determine how long it would be before I went completely blind. My husband and I stayed in a campground that winter while I underwent tests with a neuro-opthamologist.

It was December, and every afternoon the ladies would get together and knit or crochet ornaments for the Christmas tree in the clubhouse. I couldn't see to do either of those, so I made a garland by putting Christmas wrap around little one-inch squares of styrofoam, tying them with a ribbon, and stringing them on fish line. That garland hung on the Christmas tree for many years.

I didn't want to be a burden, so I borrowed a cane and learned how to get from my trailer to the clubhouse by myself at night. What a feeling of independence I had as I counted each step. It was such a small thing, but everyone celebrated with me, and I knew immediately that although total blindness might slow me down, it would never stop me from enjoying life.

I eventually found out that my loss of eyesight was due to medication I was taking. Once I stopped the medication, it took about two years to get my sight back. What a joy it was to really be able to see again!

I have asked myself many times why this happened. Was there some lesson I needed to learn? Would I have to help someone else handle the same thing some day? I finally received an answer not long ago.

I had met a woman that winter, and we had become close friends. She had a crippling disease that she knew would eventually kill her. Her husband told me last week that she had been very depressed and wanted to give up, but she found the strength to fight because of my positive attitude towards my loss of sight. She lived many happy, productive years before she died.

I am thankful every day that my eyesight was restored. I now take nothing for granted! How about you? When was the last time you really looked at a sunset? When was the last time you really looked at the trees? When did you last stop and smell a flower? When did you last listen to a bird singing?

You never know what tomorrow will bring. Are you storing up enough images for a lifetime?

- Judi Barnes

10

PATIENCE IS A VIRTUE

"A warden asked a man on death row what he would like to eat for his last meal. The inmate said, 'I would like to have a huge piece of watermelon.' The warden said, 'You must be kidding, this is December. Watermelons have not been planted, let alone harvested.' The inmate said, 'That's okay. I don't mind waiting.'"

- Larry Moyer

* * * * *

This is the story of a man in an African town. His name was Wisdom.

He had two wives (it was and still permitted to practice polygamy in many parts of Africa.) Legend had it that this man was not wealthy, despite the fact that he was a hard worker. He lived from paycheck to paycheck.

The other problem he had was that, although he had two wives, they could not bear him any children. (In most parts of Africa a man without a child was treated as an outcast.)

Wisdom did everything he could to solve these problems, all were in vain.

Then he decided to take his case to God. He prayed to God to bless him with money and children. He pleaded with God, saying that he had worked all his life but could not make ends meet. He had married two wives, hoping that at least one would bear him a child, but nothing happened.

In an answer to his prayers, God gave the man four options, from which he could choose only one. The options were:

1) *Money*
2) *Child*
3) *Patience*
4) *Longevity*

Wisdom was confused. He did not know which to choose, so he decided to confide in his wives.

The first wife opted for a child. She was so passionate that she almost convinced Wisdom to choose that option.

Wisdom decided to wait a little longer. (At times, it pays to procrastinate.) He then spoke to his younger wife. "Which should we choose?" he asked her. Immediately, the young woman said "Money." "If we have money, we can buy all the things that we lack. We will be able to have fun and enjoy ourselves," she said.

Wisdom did not choose Money. Instead, he went to his parents to consult with them on what he should choose, since he could take only one of the four options he had been given.

His parents advised him to choose Patience. Wisdom followed his parents' suggestion and went back to God. He told God he wanted to choose Patience.

God gave him Patience and took the other three options, Money, Child, and Longevity, back to heaven.

After a few years, Money called God and said, "You know, Patience is my friend and my confidant. I want to go and live with him. I can't live here alone any longer."

God released Money to go and live with Patience, who was already living with Wisdom. The poor man who had worked all his life and had no money then became rich.

One day, Child cried out to God saying, "God, you know Money and Patience are my friends, and they are no longer living with me. I want to go and live with them."

God released Child to go and live with his friends. Now Wisdom had become rich and had a child.

By now, only Longevity was left with God. One day, Longevity called God and said, "God, I'm tired of living all alone here. I want to go and live with my friends."

God released Longevity to go and live with his friends, Money, Child, and Patience.

Wisdom, who had been poor all his life, now had Patience, Money, Child and Longevity.

It's of little wonder that most successful people around the world have patience. With patience, everything will fall into place. Patience is a virtue.[1]

- Ola Joseph

---

[1] Juju music made popular by Ebenezer Obey of Nigeria.

11

IF YOU THINK YOU CAN, YOU WILL

"Perseverance is more prevailing than violence; and many things which cannot be overcome when they are together, yield themselves up when they are little by little."
- *Plutarch*

* * * * *

Often the goal is nearer than it seems to a faint and faltering man. In order to be successful and soar like an eagle, we must have the will to succeed. We must have stamina, determination and backbone, but most of all we must have perseverance and faith.

If we give up on the way, we can never know how close we are to victory.

Like commitment, we must persevere to the end, even when our interest has gone.

Many men fail because they quit too soon. They lose faith when the odds are against them. They do not have the courage to hold on and to keep fighting.

Perseverance is what makes the difference between the winner and the loser. Winners don't quit and quitters don't win.

After all is said and done, I sincerely believe that William Feather summed up perseverance best when he said, "Success seems to be largely a matter of hanging on after others have let go."

Soaring on the Wings of Courage:
The Art of Self Encouragement

Whenever you have a feeling of despair, or when everything seems to go wrong and you are about to give up, remember these occurrences in Abraham Lincoln's life. Remember that quitting is not, and should never be an option. Here is a snapshot of Abraham Lincoln's life:

Occurrence	Age
Defeated for the legislature	23
Elected to Legislature	25
Declared bankruptcy	26
His fiancée died	26
Had a nervous breakdown	26
Elected to Congress	37
Defeated for the Senate	46
Defeated for the Senate	49
Elected the President of the U.S	51

One great success can make up for many setbacks. Persevere! Never give up.

To be successful, most successful people have perseverance for breakfast, lunch, and dinner.

- Ola Joseph

12

SHAKE IT OFF AND STEP UP

"Whatever necessity lays upon thee, endure; whatever she commands, do."
- Goethe

* * * * *

An African farmer once owned an old Marjorie mule. One day the mule fell into the well on the farm. After carefully assessing the situation, the farmer concluded that it would be better to simply bury the mule in the well since it would be too much trouble for him to get him out. The mule was old anyway, thought the farmer.

He then proceeded to haul trash and dirt into the well with the intention of burying the mule there.

When the farmer realized that it was taking too long for him to do the job alone, he called his neighbors together and told them what had happened. He asked them to help haul more dirt to bury the old mule in the well and put him out of his misery.

Initially, the old mule was hysterical. But as the farmer and his neighbors continued shoveling and the dirt hit his back, a thought struck him.

It suddenly occurred to him that every time a load of dirt landed on his back, *he should shake it off, stamp on it, pack it, and step on it to step up!* This the mule did, time after time.

"Shake it off, stamp on it and step up, shake it off, stamp on it and step up, shake it off, stamp on it, pack it and step up!" he repeated to encourage himself. Even though he was in pain and distressed, the old mule fought his panic and just kept right on *shaking it off, stamping on it, packing it down, and stepping up!*

It was not long before the old mule, battered and exhausted, stepped triumphantly over the wall of the well and ran to freedom.

What seemed like it would bury him had actually blessed him, all because of the attitude with which he handled his adversity.

That's life! At some time or another, someone is going to throw trash and dirt on us. But if we have the courage to face it, to shake it off, stamp on it, pack it down, and step up, we will overcome.

The adversities that come along to bury us usually have within them the opportunities to benefit and bless us!

Endurance - shaking it off and stepping up - is a characteristic found in most successful people. They endure the nagging tongues of their friends, family members, investors, co-workers, employees, and all those who have no trust or confidence in what they are doing.

Successful people never give up, even when the going gets rough.

- Ola Joseph

13

WHOSE HOUSE AM I BUILDING?

"I can't imagine a person becoming a success who doesn't give this game of life everything he's got."
— *Walter Cronkite*

* * * * *

Successful people are not only determined to succeed, they are dependable and reliable.

The following case illustrates what dependability means and how it will make or mar your chances of soaring to the highest heights.

An elderly carpenter was ready to retire. He told his employer of his plan to leave the home building business and live a more leisurely life with his family. He would miss the paycheck, but he needed to retire. He figured that he and his family could get by.

The employer was sorry to see his good worker go, and asked if he could build just one more house as a personal favor.

The carpenter said yes, but in time it was easy to see that his heart was not in his work. Not wanting to disappoint his employer, he did everything in his power to do a good job of his last assignment. Although he was tempted on several occasions to cut corners, he resisted the temptation and delivered a near-perfect job as usual.

Well, the carpenter finished his work, and the builder came to inspect the house. When the tour of the house was over, the employer praised the carpenter for a job well done, told him he was very proud of him and thanked him for standing by him through all the years.

Then, as a token of his appreciation for all that the carpenter had done, he took the keys and handed them to the carpenter saying, "This house is a token of my appreciation. Enjoy it with your family. It is my gift. This is your house."

What a surprise! What a wonderful way to end a career! If the carpenter had not resisted the temptation to do a shoddy job, he would have regretted his actions. But because he was reliable and dependable, he put his heart into it, even when the interest was no longer there. He did his best to do a good job, and now he could live in the house he built.

So it is with us. We should build our lives in the same way.

At important points, we need to give the job our best effort. Then with a smile, we can look at the situation we have created and find that we are satisfied living in the house we built. Think of yourself as a carpenter. Think about your house. Each day you hammer in a nail, place a board, or erect a wall, build wisely.

To be successful, you have to be dependable and give your best effort, even when you are no longer interested. You never know whose house you will be building. It may be yours.

- Anonymous

14

DON'T LEAVE HOME WITHOUT IT

"Like chicken and the egg, enthusiasm and success seem to go together."
- *John Luther*

* * * * *

This is the story a captain told us when I was in the Navy. One day he was making a personal inspection of his command. Among this group was a group of Navy submariners.

When the Captain came to the group of the submariners, he asked the first man this question, "How do you like being under the sea in a submarine?"

The first sailor said, "I enjoy it very much. The hazard pay and bonus makes it especially worthwhile." The captain them proceeded to ask the second man the same question. "It's a good feeling to sneak around under the water, sir," the sailor responded. "I'd give anything to do it." "How do you like it?" the Captain asked the third man. "I don't enjoy it at all, sir," he said with alacrity. "Then why do you do it? Why do you go in the submarine?" the Captain probed further. "Because I like hanging around sailors who enjoy life under water."

No one likes being around someone who doesn't enjoy what he or she is doing, or people who are dull and uninspired. If you want to be successful, then borrow a leaf from the American Express commercial:

Soaring on the Wings of Courage:
The Art of Self Encouragement

ENTHUSIASM: DON'T LEAVE HOME WITHOUT IT.

- Ola Joseph

THE HAPPIEST AND SADDEST DAY

"Better to be prepared and not have an opportunity than to have an opportunity and not be prepared."
- Les Brown

* * * * *

Here is a story once told to me when I was in the United States Navy. It illustrates and highlights how successful people create opportunities.

Three men were riding in the Colorado Rockies on horseback one starry, moonlit night.

As they made their way along the base of the mountain, a voice thundered from the sky, commanding them to stop and dismount. They immediately followed the command.

The voice commanded, "Go to the riverbank and pick up some pebbles. Put them in your backpack and do not look at them until morning."

One of the three men who was a bit greedy, filled his backpack so much that he was unable to lift it. His friends laughed at him for being greedy. The other two only picked up a handful of pebbles.

Completing their tasks, the men began to remount when they heard the voice again. "This will be both the happiest and saddest day of your life," the voice said. With that, the men went on their way.

As the sun began to brighten up the eastern sky, the riders reached into their saddlebags. To their amazement, the pebbles had turned to gold. As they celebrated their new wealth, one of the men stopped and exclaimed, "Wait! Now I know what the voice meant when it said this would be the happiest and saddest day of our lives. Yes, we have gold, but think of how rich we would be if we had picked up more pebbles."

The man who had filled his backpack was happy, but the other two were not very happy because they had not picked up all they could.

Often people go through life and at some point think, "there could have been more." They failed to take advantage of all of the opportunities offered to them, thereby stripping themselves of unfound treasures.

Are you filling your saddlebag with every possibility and every opportunity that comes your way? If not, why not? Each day when you wake up, if you seize all the opportunities that come your way, you will be able to say "This is the happiest day of my life."

On the other hand, if you have not taken all the opportunities, you will likely say "This is the saddest day of my life."

Successful people rarely allow an opportunity to slip through their fingers. They are always prepared, even when there is no opportunity at the moment, so when an opportunity comes, they are ready to take it.

Most of the time successful people create the opportunity they want, even if none exists.

- Anonymous

TEACH A CHILD THE WAY HE SHOULD GO

"Discipline is the foundation upon which all success is built. Lack of discipline inevitably leads to failure."

- Jim Rohn

* * * * *

I started my high school sophomore year in a small downtown Catholic school named St. Joseph. At that time I did not realize the effect the principal of the school would have on the rest of my life, and the type of discipline she sometimes used.

One of the first students I met was a tall, slim, black haired, cigarette-smoking, pool-playing Irishman by the name of James Whitcombe Riley (no relation to the poet). He was certainly not a candidate for class valedictorian.

Riley, however, did have some interesting skills. Riley knew how to slip into the back door of the Criterion Theatre; he knew how to ride the public transportation system free, and in the language of the pool hall, Riley shot a pretty good stick.

This latter skill was what first got me into trouble. I came back about five minutes late from lunch hour break, and the principal, Sister Margaret Mary was waiting in the hall.

She was a little Irish nun, with a face that looked like it was chiselled from granite and pale blue eyes that could see right through the four-inch armor plate of the Battleship Texas.

"Young man, why are you late?" Now one of the first things I had learned was that you did not lie to Sister Margaret Mary. Your tongue would fall off.

So I looked into those pale blues, and said, "I went down to Ray's club, to play pool."

"And does your mother know that you play pool with the likes of James Whitcombe Riley?"

"Well, she, ah, ... knows I play."

"I see. Go to your room," she said firmly.

I went to my room, with the feeling that that was not the end of the conversation. I knew my mother would hear about it and therefore it would resume when I arrived home.

However, everything was normal that evening, and when nothing further happened the following day, I forgot about it.

Then Friday rolled around. It was a beautiful spring day. The Oklahoma Indians were playing an exhibition game that afternoon. Riley and another stalwart by the name of Timothy Bradshaw walked up to me.

"Stan, we're going to cut class, and go to the baseball game. Would you like to come?"

"I don't have any money."

"You won't need any," he said.

So that afternoon I learned how to ride the public transportation system free, and I also learned how to get into the ball game free.

My only concern was whether I would be missed at school, and if so, how long it would take them to call my home.

Again when I arrived home, conditions were normal. When nothing happened Monday morning, I realized I had cut class for the first time and gotten away with it.

The rest of the week was uneventful until Thursday morning. I awakened to the sound of a real Oklahoma downpour. It was the type that would make Noah very nervous.

By the time I had showered and had breakfast, it was raining even harder, so I asked my mother if she would take me to school. She said okay, but I might be a few minutes late. No problem, I thought.

I arrived about 10 minutes late, and who was there to greet me? Sister Margaret Mary. "Young man, why are you late?"

"Well Sister, because of the rain. I had to wait for my mother to take me to school."

"And did you have to wait for your mother to take you to the ball game Friday afternoon?"

"Well I, ah."

"Go to your room," she said

I went to my room, fully realizing that I was not as smart as I had thought. I also prepared myself for what I was sure to get at home. But once more, nothing happened at home.

Soaring on the Wings of Courage:
The Art of Self Encouragement

The next afternoon, when recess time arrived, I was told to report to Sister Margaret Mary's office. Upon entering, I saw her sitting behind a large, clean desk, which was intimidating in itself. She was holding a manuscript of some sort.

"In six weeks there is going to be a city wide youth rally, and we have to furnish a speaker for that rally. I want you to be that speaker." Even though I had never done any speaking, I immediately came up with five or six good reasons why she would be better off finding someone else.

Despite this, she looked me straight in the eye and said. "I want you to be that speaker." I suddenly realized that it was payback time. "Take this manuscript home with you and memorize it. Be prepared to work on it Monday morning."

When Monday arrived, I had a fair working knowledge of that speech, and that afternoon, when everyone else took a recess break, I reported to Sister Margaret Mary's office to work on the speech.

That routine continued for four weeks, then I sort of graduated, and was sent to Father MacGoldrick, to work on things like voice variation, pauses, eye contact, etc.

My mother questioned this. "Why Father MacGoldrick? He has enough trouble keeping his teeth in place when he speaks." However, after two weeks of Father MacGoldrick, I was pronounced ready.

The rally was set for 8:00 P.M. Friday. I got up that morning with no appetite, and that feeling was with me throughout the day.

I don't remember how I arrived at the auditorium, but I remember standing in the wings at about 8:05 P.M., and hearing an announcement. I didn't get it all, but I did hear, "St Joseph High School," and "Stan Flanagan," and I knew I was on. I also knew I had two choices, I could hide, or I could die.

Once I chose to die, the adrenaline began to pump. I walked up to the lectern, laid the speech in front of me, and began. I never looked once at the speech, but delivered it with all the voice variation, pauses, and eye contact that we had worked on over the past six weeks. At the end, the audience applauded, and I discovered that I liked that feeling.

Sister Margaret Mary has long since gone on to be with her creator, and I have no idea what happened to Riley.

I found out later that Sister Margaret Mary had a knack for handling problems, and her solution to each one was unique.

I do know this: she saw a need for me to be on the platform long before I did. She inspired me to give more presentations.

Now, when I finish a presentation and the audience applauds, I can almost feel her presence as she says, "Young man, go to your room." We could use a lot more Sister Margaret Marys today.

- Stan Flanagan

17

ASK NOT WHAT GOD CAN DO FOR YOU

"I've stopped expecting you to make leaps of faith, but it would be nice to see a hop now and then."
- Doug Hall

* * * * *

I believe that my faith is the reason for my success and the success yet to come. I wish I had delegated my worries to God years ago.

At the age of 30 I lost the use of my arms and legs. I remember in rehab thinking (not praying) that if I could just have the use of my arms I would be able to do everything I needed.

I didn't need to walk - I needed to be able to run the wheelchair, drive, comb my hair, and feed myself. I was mentally bargaining. It worked. Unknown to me then, God was working in my life. But I didn't see the angels around me that included the doctors, rehab personnel and friends. I believed that it was I who overcame the situation - my power of positive thinking, drive, mind over body. Not until later did I realize that I was working myself to death, not taking care of myself, because I wouldn't slow down. So God picked me up, and put me in the hospital because I couldn't take care of me. I felt a message, but I didn't get it.

Once healed, I went right back into that hard working world where I was always a success. ME racing against ME. I valued my friends, but I didn't need anyone.

I traveled 13 states and worked all the time. Moving up the ladder, that's what it was all about! So I thought. I'm not sure I could have defined happiness,- but I could define my idea of success.

Then at the age of 48, following my third divorce and in the midst of a demanding job, I slowed down long enough to feel loneliness. I also found a drive to hang out in places where no one knew me and where people thought I was the greatest. I then found stress relief in a beer bottle.

After 4 months of emotionally hiding, a significant event happened in my life that changed it forever.

I found myself in my moving car on a dark, deserted stretch of road, no lights anywhere, at 3:00 o'clock in the morning. I had absolutely no idea where I was or how I had gotten there. I felt true fear for the first time.

Then I said "Oh God, please help me." I guess I picked up my cell phone and dialed a number - all I know is I began talking to a man from Pearland, Texas. I had no idea who he was - he had no idea who I was. Neither of us has been able to figure out how I phoned him. I believe I thought I was dialing a friend's number and God crossed the wires and connected me to this man.

He was a disabled veteran and an alcoholic. He thought my call was a joke. I was crying so hard he realized it was not. He woke up his roommate and they got a map to try and help me.

As I became more aware of my situation, embarrassed, I hung up. I could figure this out. I knew how to be in control. I could manage. Then more fear went through me like a cold wind. I had sense enough to press redial, and after 1.5 hours of encouragement, this stranger talked me home to a place he had never been.

The stranger quit drinking that night. So did I. I changed his life and he changed mine. We both believe God put us together. I was his angel. He was mine. All for a reason.

I continued to excel and grow in my career. I was a Human Resource Manager in charge of Employee Development & Organizational Effectiveness. I had been with the firm for 14 years.

Then at 53 years of age, I asked God to help me through another difficult period. Work wasn't fun or interesting any more. My staff was doing the kinds of work I wanted to do. I had continued to be promoted farther away from "the people," and spent all of my time reading reports or going to meetings. I missed doing the very things I loved. It wasn't exciting to go to work any more. It wasn't enough.

On the way to work the next morning, I noticed a church marquee that said, "When growth stops, decay begins." God answered my prayer through that sign. I walked into work and signed papers allowing me to retire after 14 years with the company. I put my house on the market, left my friends, and moved to Houston without a job.

All of that came with a sense of calm and peace I never had before. I now own my own business. I am booked for the next four months. I haven't advertised or finished developing my brochure. For every question or fear I have had, God has answered.

I am doing what I have a passion to do. I am using the gifts God gave me. I am learning to listen to find out what it is HE wants me to do now. I have learned He has always been there - I just have not always been willing to listen.

My faith in God makes me successful. Many people come and go in my life, but HE is always with me.

I ask you this: is there room for growth in your life? Remember, "When growth stops - decay begins."

Challenge yourself. Reach out. Don't be afraid of growth. Do what you love to do, and the joy will follow.

Ask not what God can do for you. Ask God, "What can I do with the gifts you've given me?"

- Pamela Smith

18

SUCCESS IS A JOURNEY

"There is much in the world to make us afraid. There is much more in our faith to make us unafraid."
- *Frederick W. Cropp*

* * * * *

Many years ago, I learned the true power of God and having faith. My cousin Hector had everything going for him. He was 17, had a good Catholic family, was an athlete and was handsome. Various football team agents had been approaching him with scholarships.

Hector was the eldest of my Aunt Julia and Uncle Luis' two natural-born children. He had a younger sister, Belinda. My aunt and uncle also had two adopted younger children, Christopher and Gina.

All was well for the family and all were prospering. Hector and I were growing up together. He was just three and half years older than I, and we had played together since we were children.

Then one day Hector became very ill. He was diagnosed with leukemia. The family was devastated. My aunt was the most affected by the news. She loved all her children, but Hector was the inspiration for the family. I remember seeing even my father cry as he explained to us what leukemia was.

We were all raised as Catholics and believed in God. Our faith was strong, along with our values. I guess I never expected that our faith would be put through such a test.

I can remember the day I first saw Hector in the hospital. Even with all the tubes, he kept his sense of humor. Well, the leukemia spread quickly and the doctors soon informed my aunt and uncle that there was no hope for Hector. He had just turned 18. My dad, being the strongest of all the children in his family, had to remind my aunt and the rest of his brothers and sisters how strong prayer could be.

Hector's body had deteriorated. I remember squeezing his arm and feeling only a water-like texture. There was no muscle left. One day my aunt was told that the Pope was coming to Mexico. Without a thought, my aunt and father said that Hector must be taken there to be blessed. My aunt and uncle's financial status was shaky by this time with all the medical bills. Nevertheless, they spent every dime they had taking Hector to see the Pope. My dad was also a big contributor to the cause. Like most teenagers, I didn't understand why our vacation money and college savings were being given away. My dad's answer was always, "the good Lord provides as necessary."

So my aunt and Hector ventured off in an ambulance to Mexico, even though she was advised not to take him. The doctors felt the long ride and the trip would surely take his life.

I don't remember the time period exactly. Perhaps it was just a couple of weeks, or maybe a month, but my cousin Hector got well. I remember seeing him starting to walk again, smile again and be teased again.

Hector went through many years of radiation therapy, and even a kidney transplant. Belinda, his sister, gave him one of her kidneys without a second thought.

Hector went on to college and obtained a bachelor's degree. Then he went on to MIT and graduated with a master's degree at age 33. Even though he had a master's degree in computer science, he worked for a local non-profit organization helping native Spanish-speaking children learn to read.

Hector is now in heaven. He died at 37 of a heart attack. We were all sad that such a wonderful person died so young. The one comforting thing I remember is my aunt saying to me, "Rose Marie, I will miss Hector so much, especially his talking with me, and the way he made me laugh. I thank God for allowing him to stay with me those additional 20 years, and that I was able to live to see him develop into a real man."

- Rose Nolen

19

THE SPRINGBOARD OF LIFE

"It takes strength to use the past as an anchor; it takes courage to use it as a springboard."
- Ola Joseph

* * * * *

Does life sometimes seem overwhelming? Do you feel at times that you are carrying the Empire State Building around on your shoulders? If so, you are definitely not alone.

At the age of twenty-six I was the proud mother of four beautiful children, the youngest being a set of twins.

There is no need to elaborate on my lack of sleep. I was up all day and all night.

Like many young families, money was definitely not in abundance. I soon learned to be creative, especially when it came to meals.

The chance to live in Europe and Southeast Asia seemed to come at just the right moment in my life. It brought a wealth of educational opportunities and the rewards of close and permanent friendships.

Are you now picturing in your mind's eye the move across the world with four young children, thinking, "She couldn't possibly find the courage to do such a thing?" Sure I could. When opportunity knocks, you open the door.

Soaring on the Wings of Courage:
The Art of Self Encouragement

The emotional pressures of life did not vanish with the move, but I embraced and learned from every minute of this wonderful experience. Making Houston, Texas home after over ten years of living overseas was a big adjustment for all of us. Houston seemed more like a small country than a city, and feeling our way around was a big challenge.

Within a couple of years, the children were all grown and on their own, or away at college. About the same time, I was diagnosed with a non-fatal but painful chronic illness. It didn't take long before I felt like the tin man in disguise.

Added to my empty nest syndrome and the illness, my family business plummeted along with the Houston economy.

Here I was on my own, my home so quiet you could hear a pin drop. Yet not too long ago, it was filled with noisy, hungry teenagers.

Have you ever felt so alone that your self-esteem was about as low as it can get? Well cheer up. You do not hold a patent on those feelings. I and many others have had these same feelings at one time or another.

The climb up is not always an easy one, but it is a worthwhile one. We all have choices, which, I must admit, I wasn't aware of for a long time. Now I had the choice of becoming a recluse or taking control of my life. I chose life.

Taking control and making changes wasn't easy, but getting a full life was worth all the hard work and effort.

By joining a gym, swimming, exercising, and praying everyday, and by taking proper mediations, my future began to look brighter.

I also attended a self-help meeting almost every night for a long time. I cannot possibly express just how much this helped me get a better handle on my life.

Joining Toastmasters International was another decision that helped me beyond words. My childhood dreams were to be a mother and a public speaker.

Because I didn't have boundaries, I too often let other people control me, but as soon as I changed, the world around me changed.

Do you sometimes feel you can't possibly climb out of the hole you're stuck in? Again, you're not feeling anything others haven't felt.

My self-esteem was soon way above sea level. I realized I could only learn from the past, not change it. I used my new-found knowledge to keep moving forward, and I continued to create more balance and happiness in my life.

My goal is to help others take the shorter road and never feel their dream is beyond reach.

In my search, I found the National Speakers Association, where my dream has become a reality. And to think I almost let it get away.

Thanks also go to my children, grandchildren, and my friends for all of their encouragement and support of my dreams.

If we remember to use the past as a springboard and not as an anchor, the sky will be the limit.

GOD BLESS, and never give up on your dream, regardless of how impossible it may seem.

- Rae Broussard

20

MOTHER IS SUPREME

"When you see the world only through your own eyes, you tend to think that other people are myopic."
- Ola Joseph

* * * * *

It has been said that by the time you realize your parents were right, you have your own children who think you are wrong.

Some of us are so full of ourselves that we think our parents' ideas are obsolete. Many times we brush aside their words of wisdom, thinking they aren't worth our trouble to listen to.

But alas, here is a story to show that the words of our elders are words of wisdom. Mother is supreme after all.

I was standing in the bookstore randomly skimming through books to find that catchy phrase that sells, when I came upon it.

A quote from LynEllen, "Our mothers ought to know how to push our buttons – they were the ones who installed them." That was it! I couldn't get to the counter quickly enough to add this book to my self-help library.

My relationship with my mother had always been a tenuous one. She was a perfectionist in denial, and I was a slob in defiance. She was externally motivated while I was internally motivated. It seemed as though we had no common ground upon which to build a close relationship.

Mother was adamant that my father and I should look and act perfectly at all times, according to Emily Post's guidelines. This was the basis of everyone's opinion of you, according to my mother.

Her philosophy was often difficult to buy for a daughter who would rather be honing her four position, .22 caliber skills, and 50-foot indoor shooting ability. My mother's continual comments on my appearance grew to be interpreted as criticism very early in my youth. The hot buttons had been installed.

As the years progressed, my mother's comments continued to create personal turmoil within me, unleashing uncontrollable emotional reactions that caused much hurt between us.

As far as I could tell, she placed no value on my personal achievements or my business success. She was only concerned with my appearance and observance of the social graces. As I turned 40, our times together were still difficult, until November 5, 1992 when my mother suffered a stroke. She was paralyzed on her right side and could not speak, read, write, or swallow.

Over the next two months of rehabilitation, I saw a side of my mother I was never open-minded enough to recognize. Inside that opinionated person was a woman committed and determined to overcoming her barriers to living.

As she regained her mobility, began to eat again, and speak a few words, her perseverance never waned. I grew to know her better over the following years, and learned that the personal values she was so committed to had been self-taught.

I began to admire her passion and dedication, even if she continued to test those hot buttons.

I have learned two life lessons from my mother. First, if you believe in something, don't ever compromise that belief. Mother continues to be committed to her self-taught values, teaching me to have confidence in my opinions. Second, you can be strong in your commitment without being judgmental.

My mother continues to comment on my appearance, but understanding her motivation now makes me ask: "Who was misunderstood?"

- *Linda Stiles*

PLAYING TO WIN OR PLAYING NOT TO LOSE?

"Our aspirations are our possibilities."
- *Robert Browning*

* * * * *

Are you playing to win or playing not to lose?

In 1989 Nigeria and Russia played in the finals of the Junior World Cup Soccer Competition.

The Russians had a lead at half time. But the Nigerian team came out after halftime and battled the Russians. With about ten minutes left in the match, the Nigerians were still three goals down, but they kept the spirit up. They continued their mass attack and mass defense strategy, and in fact, they scored three goals in less than five minutes and went on to win the match.

What happened in that match? Well, I think the Russians changed their game plan during the second half of the match. They went from a position of playing to win, to playing not to lose. But the Nigerians went from playing not to lose to playing to win.

How often do we do this in our life? We will have a job that pays a good salary with a 401K plan, and we will have been there for at least ten years. We think that if we can just hold out for five to ten more years we can retire. Then we can really start to have fun and enjoy our days more. We are playing not to lose – not playing to win.

Many people go to work and can't wait for the weekend to come. They are wishing for the day to go by, a day that they will never see again. A lot of people have pains that are related to stress brought on by their jobs. They hate what they are doing, but because it pays good money they do not leave. They dislike their supervisor or really dislike their co-workers, but they remain there. Their job may be very boring and burning them out, but they continue to stay, hoping something will happen to bring them happiness. Such people should consider changing jobs or get training for a new career, but they don't because they are playing not to lose, rather than playing to win.

A good friend of mine in her 50s is self-employed and very successful. She has to do a lot of traveling on her job and the physical aspects of her job are beginning to wear her out. But instead of thinking to herself "how can I keep what I have accumulated and retire?" Her position is "what can I do now to start a new career?" She is working on starting a new business, using the money she has accumulated to start it. She is a great example of someone playing to win.

In order to play to win, you need a lot of energy, great attitude and impeccable enthusiasm. If you are burned out or just getting by, this takes away a lot of your energy. What you have to do first is have a change of attitude, then set a goal and have a timeline. With a goal in mind you can focus more on what you want to work on. The more you concentrate on your goal, the more motivation you will have. You do not always have to leave your present company, sometimes a new position will give you a whole new outlook.

Olayinka Joseph

Playing to win is not about making a lot of money, it is about doing what makes you feel like you are accomplishing what is important to you. It is about fulfilling your purpose in life. You need to like what you are doing and not dread it. More importantly, what you are doing must benefit the human race.

Playing to win usually means taking more risks, but there is also a great satisfaction in knowing you have at least tried. Remember, lack of courage and will power have caused more failure than lack of intelligence and ability.

- *Joan Bolling/Ola Joseph*

HE THAT IS IN US

"Faith is kept alive in us, and gathers strength, more from practice than from speculations."
― *Joseph Addison*

* * * * *

She wouldn't use the term "successful" to describe herself. If I called her "courageous" or a "risk-taker," she would laugh and shake her head in disagreement. I can imagine my little sister Lori smiling and saying, "Lynnie, I just ask God what He wants me to do. I listen, and I do it. It is not always easy, but it is really pretty simple. Want some more coffee?"

I certainly agree with the "not easy" part, and as I grow in my own faith, I understand more about the "simple" part. Lori has moved through her amazing life with humility, compassion, and a resilience that she doesn't always recognize. I admire today what I used to secretly envy-her willingness to take huge leaps of faith, with the rock-solid belief that God will manage all the details she can't yet see.

Perhaps not every risk she has taken over her 42 years has been blessed by heaven. When she was four, Lori threw a bucket of sand at the sliding glass door when the babysitter was cramping her style. I didn't care much for this woman either, but my risk-averse self suffered in silence. I secretly applauded Lori's courageous form of protest, but I think I abandoned her in the hour of judgment!

I usually got better grades in school, but I understood how to win in that system. I certainly worked hard, and my teachers were predictably pleased with my efforts and dedication, but I never stretched beyond what I knew I could master. Lori would consistently get involved in subjects and activities that tested her limits. She took physiology with the dreaded Mr. "D," swim team, drill team and other rigorous and demanding classes that were not necessarily areas of natural talent for her. She didn't always win, but she made those experiences a win for everyone in her circle.

In addition to my straight A's, I was considered the creative child in our family. But one day when I was in high school, I was cleaning out some shelves in our basement and discovered a box of Lori's drawings and essays from her 1st grade year. Inventive, heartfelt, and thoroughly original, they far surpassed anything I had or would ever produce.

Lori yearned for life beyond Ohio, and spent her college summers in far-flung spots like Yellowstone, and the Grand Canyon, and remote regions of Montana. In typical fashion, she would get there first, and then figure out how she was going to support herself. She developed a passion for places of wild and rugged beauty. I spent my summers sewing in the basement of my parents' home in Dayton.

Lori settled in California after struggling through nursing school, and became a nurse in the intensive care unit at UC Davis Medical Center. There were so many other safer, less traumatic positions available, and yet she was pulled once again to live at the outer limits of her learning.

UC Davis was the destination, often the final destination, for victims of the worst traffic accidents, drug overdoses and violent lifestyles.

Although these patients had far less than a 50% chance of survival, and many of them were less than sympathetic characters, Lori brought courage and compassion to every patient she encountered.

Dealing daily with suffering and death had hardened many of her fellow nurses, and they did not support Lori's efforts to connect with her patients. Without intending to, she had raised the standard of care. Her warmth and openness forced them to confront the callousness they had developed, thinking it would shield them from the gut-wrenching disappointment of losing patients. As the years went by the callousness dissipated, but it wasn't until Lori resigned that the nurses shared with her how much she had softened their hearts simply through her loving, non-judgmental presence.

It was during her difficult nursing years that Lori became a "born-again" Christian. We had been raised in a wonderful, typical, Midwest Catholic family. Her newfound faith was met with raised eyebrows and quiet disdain, thinly disguised as curiosity. When I wasn't openly confrontational with her, I was dismissive and arrogant. In fact, I felt rejected by her in some odd way. She was hurt by her family's lack of enthusiasm, but she stayed true to her beliefs and continued to love us through our frustrations and adjustments to her new way of life.

When Lori would talk openly about her faith, I could argue with her from an intellectual standpoint. But when I watched her live her faith, I was rattled to my core. She broke off an engagement to a wonderful and wealthy man who loved her immensely, but did not share her beliefs and had no interest in pursuing a spiritual path. I knew how much she loved him and would miss having him in her life, and I could not understand her logic. Even more disturbing to me was the realization that I did not have her courage. I would not have sacrificed love for my faith. Lori was able to quiet the voices in her head and heart and seek direction from a deeper, wiser source.

Months later, after much loneliness but no regrets, she called my parents from California, asking them to help find her a good Christian man. The very next day, while attending mass in their Dayton, Ohio church, my parents spotted a handsome young man sitting with his family. Amazed by their own boldness, they approached John after the service and invited him to brunch. He accepted as a courtesy, and found himself patiently and politely viewing family photo albums at their home later that day.

John had recently relocated to Dayton, purchased a condo, and was getting established in his position with a nationally recognized corporation—why in the world would he pursue a relationship with a girl thousands of miles away? Again, as a courtesy, he called my sister. That first phone call was two hours long. She appreciated the call, but was disappointed to learn that his faith was a very small part of his life. He was intrigued and disturbed, wanting to know more about this unusual young woman of courage and conviction. They married less than two years later. The orchestration of this incredible love story was a clear indicator of God's hand at work—just one of many miracles that have since unfolded in Lori's life.

After struggling with years of infertility, John and Lori began looking into adopting a child. God brought Caleb into Lori and John's life when he was less than two days old. Prayerful consideration was immediately followed by a courageous leap of faith, and they moved forward to begin adoption proceedings.

When Caleb was just two months old, Lori discovered she was pregnant with her daughter, Amy Lynn. On Veterans Day in 1994, Lori had an emergency C-section, during which the anesthesiologist administered the paralytic drug, but neglected to spot a kink in the tube that delivered the anesthetic. She was fully conscious for the operation, and felt every cut of the surgeon's knife, but was unable to move or speak. Her trauma, however, quickly became a secondary concern, because Amy was near death.

When my mother called me from the San Antonio hospital that Friday night, I was expecting a joyful report with descriptions of eyes, hair, weight, and length. I was not at all prepared to learn that Amy had been born with severe meconium poisoning—that her tiny lungs were completely clogged with a greenish-black muck that had contaminated the amniotic fluid during the 48 hours prior to her birth.

At her appointment early that morning, Lori's OB/Gyn had dismissed the baby's irregular heartbeat as a matter of little concern. In fact, it was a matter of life and death. By that time Amy had been struggling for oxygen for almost a day. The doctor didn't miss it—he *dis*missed it, and he later falsified the records to cover up his poor decision.

The doctors at the hospital were not hopeful about Amy's chances for survival, and were even less optimistic about her quality of life should she somehow make it through the night. They reported that they had never seen a baby born alive with meconium poisoning at this level of severity. Amy was the only full-term baby in the neo-natal intensive care unit, but the most critically ill.

Because I was suffering from pleurisy, I was distressed to learn that even if I disobeyed my doctor's orders and traveled to San Antonio, I would not be allowed around Lori or Amy. I was finally able to reach Lori by phone from Houston on Saturday afternoon. Her anguish left me heartsick and weak with worry, but her unwavering faith empowered me. Although exhausted and in shock from her own horrific surgery, she tearfully, yet very peacefully told me that she was prepared to give Amy back to God. I don't think she could have possibly imagined or prepared for the harrowing events she and her family would endure over the next three months.

That Sunday I marched into the church I had been attending on a very irregular basis. On previous visits I had occasionally wandered into Bible study prior to the service, although sitting through the endless prayer requests that preceded the lesson always made me uncomfortable. I had always thought of prayer as an intensely private affair, and it seemed almost voyeuristic to me to be listening in on other people's problems. That Sunday, however, I stuffed every bit of pride, pretense, and propriety I had ever harbored and asked those total strangers in Bible study to pray for my sister and her dying baby.

Finding the courage to make that simple prayer request marked a turning point in my life. It might not have qualified as a risk in anyone else's book, but it was a major risk for me on many levels, and in ways I didn't fully understand until years later. I risked my safe position as an anonymous, silent observer in this community of outspoken believers. I risked the embarrassment of exposing emotions I wasn't sure I could contain or control. I risked opening myself up again to a God who hadn't bothered to answer any of my prayers in what seemed like years. Nevertheless, on the slim chance that it might save my niece, I was determined to enlist the prayers of every soul in that room. It was more than a risk…it was a leap of faith. I left the service that day emptied of pride, yet full of peace. I knew in my bones that God would heal Amy.

Amy continued to survive, but she did not thrive. Although Amy had generally competent care, Lori's experience as an intensive care nurse allowed her to catch a critical oversight in Amy's blood oxygen level on a particularly difficult and busy day for the nursing staff. Upon reporting the situation, Lori was told to mind her own business and let the professionals do their jobs. Her faith in God remained unshaken even as she lost faith in the people upon whom her daughter's life depended. With His help she fought for the very best care team available. Right before Christmas, a desperate, high-risk decision was made by this team to remove a major section of Amy's lung, a decision that saved her life.

Amy's homecoming a month later was bittersweet. The doctors prepared Lori and John for the responsibilities they would face as the parents of a weak, sickly, high-maintenance child. Amy would be unable to leave the confines of home until at least 8 years of age, due to the chronic respiratory problems she was sure to experience. They discussed the likelihood of learning disabilities, a result of her intermittent oxygen deprivation and extended dependence on a respirator. There were also legitimate concerns about her developing attachment disorder, since no one was able to hold Amy during her first three months of life.

When I see Amy today, six years later, her barely visible scars still have the power to transport me back to that awful period, but it is a quick trip. The only thing that makes Amy weak and sick these days is the prospect of picking up her clothes and toys! Amy washes her little hands fifty times a day, but not because she has to follow some strict health guidelines—she just doesn't like to have sticky fingers!

Amy never spent a single day indoors when she wanted to be outside, and she is as smart, sweet, and stubborn as you'd expect any 6-year-old to be. She is the talk of the town, the belle of the ball, Daddy's girl, and Caleb's best friend. She told me last week that she loves school, but sometimes she really misses her Mommy during the day. Best of all, she lavishes her Aunt Lynn with affection. She thinks I'm very fun and that I dress fancy! So much for attachment disorder.

Amy doesn't know how God protected her little life even as He used the miraculous events of her conception, birth, and recovery to save and change countless other lives, including mine. One day she will be told her story in its entirety. I imagine that she'll marvel as I do at how God covered every mistake made and managed every detail.

Soaring on the Wings of Courage:
The Art of Self Encouragement

As for my sister's "story"-the Amy chapter, the Caleb chapter, the John chapter, and the California chapter-these are but representative samples of her remarkable life. I have left many chapters untold, and in the chapter currently unfolding, God is at it again! He leads, she follows. With Lori's faith and full cooperation, He continues to impact many lives through the dramatic events He places in her life.

Does it take courage to put God fully in charge of your life? I think so. But Lori is convinced that it takes less courage to follow God's plan than it does to navigate your own plan without Him at the helm. However, when I think of the risks she has taken for Him, and the paths He has asked her to walk, I must admit that He scares me! What will He ask *me* to do, and will He bless me with the courage and faith to do it?

She says her life is simple—not risky, not courageous, not successful in a way that the world understands. We can agree to disagree about her personal attributes, but she will never convince me that she is not a "success." Of the many successful people I've worked with in my career, my little sister Lori lives the most successful life.

Ask…listen…follow His lead. Maybe success really is that simple.

- Lynn Schoener

Olayinka Joseph

Other Contributors

Carol Taylor is a freelance writer living in Golden Colorado.

Pamela Smith has been in management and training for over 20 years. At the age of 53 she took advantage of an early retirement offer. She sold her house, packed up, and moved to Houston, Texas where she and has started her own training company, Strategic Choices, Inc.

David S. Teachout retired as a Navy Captain after a 34- year career. Following retirement he graduated from Western State College of Law and eventually passed the California bar. He is currently serving as the Manager, Workers' Compensation for Sharp Healthcare in San Diego, California. He resides in Coronado with his wife Mary. Dave and Mary are blessed with four sons and nine grandchildren.

Judi Barnes is a member of Escapees Toastmasters Club, Livingston, Texas.

Linda Stiles is the Director of Business Applications for Transocean Sedco-Forex and lives in West Houston with her husband, Joe and their dog, Max.

Stan Flanagan is a professional speaker who specializes in sales training, and consultation.

Nadine Galinsky is an author, editor, and owner of Gal-In- Sky Publishing Company, which is dedicated to publishing works that make a positive contribution to the world. She lives in Houston, Texas, with her husband, Jim, and several furry friends.

Rose Nolen is a Sr. Human Resources Advisor/Corporate Recruiter for Dynegy Marketing and Trade in Houston, Texas. She lives with her husband Paul, their son, John Luke Nolen and two dogs, Sparky and Zen. Rose continues to engage in many volunteer activities. Her faith remains strong. She is always reaching out to touch others' lives.

Olayinka Joseph

Renata L. Nero, Ph.D., lives in Houston, Texas. She is an associate professor of psychology at a small private university in Houston, Texas. In her spare time she participates in Toastmasters and enjoys gardening and spending time with her family.

Lynn Schoener is an Executive & Team Coach based in Houston, Texas. She speaks, trains, writes, and consults nationwide on the issues of change and renewal. In September of 2000, Lynn celebrated 20 years in the field of Training & Organizational Development, and 20 years of marriage to her high-school sweetheart and coach, John.

OTHER TITLES BY OLAYINKA JOSEPH

Voices Of Courage – Everyone Has a Story

To order Voices of Courage-Everyone Has a Story click here to go to www.olayinka.com.

Soaring on the Wings of Courage:
The Art of Self Encouragement

ORDER FORM

For additional copies of this book, please send e-mail/or your request to ola.talks@olayinka.com the address below or visit www.olayinka.com

Golden Heart Books
P.O.Box 721791, Houston, TX 77272-1791
Tel: (713) 283-5141, Toll Free: 1-800-522-1970
Fax: (775) 665-8521

# Copies	**Price**	**U.S. Shipping/Handling**
1 Paperback	$13.95 each	$4.00 First book/CD
1 (Hard Cover)	$17.95 each	$3.50 each add. book

10 + copies (20% discount)   50 + copies (40% discount)

International Orders Shipping/handling:
Surface: $20.00 for the first book/CD/Tape,
               $12.00 each additional book

Please no COD Orders

..... of books x cost per book = total $............
Shipping/handling $............
Texas residents add 8.25% sales tax $............
           Grand Total $
                                           ========

Payment: Check: ....   Amount $...............
Credit Card: VISA,   MC,   AMEX,   DISC

Card No. .... Exp. Date ....
Name on Card: ....Sign...............

Shipping Address:
Name: _____
Shipping Address:_____
City: _____State: _____Zip:_____
Telephone (   )_____ Ext: _____

Olayinka Joseph

ABOUT THE AUTHOR

Olayinka Joseph, president of Riverbank & Associates (Riverbank Seminars) is an inspirational speaker, corporate trainer, author, and consultant. He delivers over 30 speeches a year to audiences numbering from 10 to 1500. He inspires his audiences in the areas of Communications, Personal Growth, Self-Improvement, and Empowerment.

Born on an island village of less than 600 inhabitants, Ola arrived in the United States a few years ago with less than $100 in his pocket believing that the most important ingredient to success is courage. Having the courage to take action even when it appears the outcome may not be favorable.

Coming from a background of almost nothingness to making something of himself has taken a lot of faith, perseverance, and courage.

Ola attended Lagos City College and Yaba College of Technology, Lagos Nigeria. After college, he worked with Total, Mobil, Texaco, and First City Merchant Bank before moving to the United States and later joined the United States Navy.

Ola holds a Bachelor of Arts degree in Legal Studies and a Master of Arts degree in Human Resources Management.

Ola is a member of the National Speakers Association and The Association of Human Resources Professionals. He has served on the board of the Houston Chapter of NSA as the Membership Committee Chairperson and has served as an Area Governor with Toastmasters International.

Soaring on the Wings of Courage is his second book.